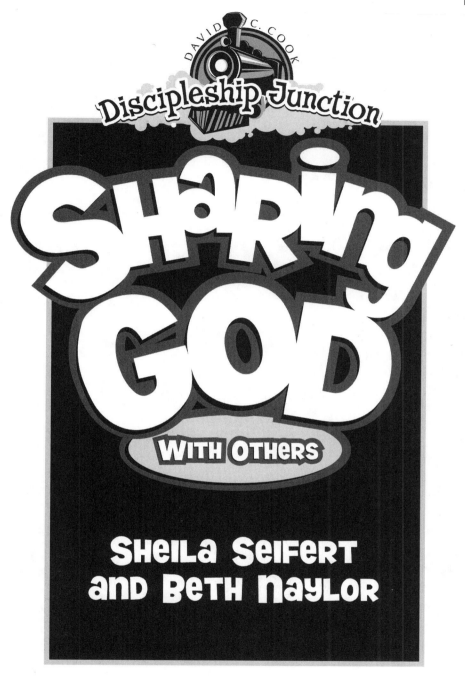

DAVID C. COOK
Discipleship Junction

Sharing GOD
With Others

Sheila Seifert
and Beth Naylor

NEXGEN®

Building the New Generation of Believers

COOK COMMUNICATIONS MINISTRIES
Colorado Springs, Colorado • Paris, Ontario
KINGSWAY COMMUNICATIONS LTD
Eastbourne, England

NexGen® is an imprint of
Cook Communications Ministries
Colorado Springs, CO 80918
Cook Communications, Paris, Ontario
Kingsway Communications, Eastbourne, England

SHARING GOD WITH OTHERS
© 2007 by Cook Communications Ministries

Cover Design: BMB Design
Cover Illustration: BMB Design/Ryan Putnam
Interior Design: TrueBlue Design/Sandy Flewelling
Interior Illustrations: Aline Heiser

First Printing 2007
Printed in the United States

1 2 3 4 5 6 7 8 9 10 Printing/Year 11 10 09 08 07

ISBN 978-0-7814-4443-9
104957

Table of Contents

WELCOME TO
DISCIPLESHIP JUNCTION!

Discipleship Junction is an all-new program that harnesses the power of FUN to build young disciples through interaction with Bible truth and with each other.

A complete, multi-age children's ministry program, *Discipleship Junction* is packed full of interactive stories and drama, Scripture memory, and themed snacks and activities that will engage every child! It is guaranteed effective because its principles and methods of instruction are *teacher-tested* and *kid-approved*!

Intensive student-teacher interaction within a learning community that is relational and supportive makes *Discipleship Junction* an ideal program for including children with disabilities. Hands-on learning activities are easily adapted to include all students. For more ideas about inclusion, an excellent resource is *Let All the Children Come to Me* by MaLesa Breeding Ed.D., Dana Hood, Ph.D., and Jerry Whitworth, Ed.D., (Colorado Springs: Cook Communication Ministries, 2006).

Putting the Pieces Together

Get Set. We know you're busy, so we provide a list of materials and what you'll need to prepare for your lesson. You'll also need a photocopy machine and some basic classroom supplies: paper, pencils, markers, butcher paper, scissors, glue and index cards. When you see this icon ⏱ allow a little extra prep time.

Tickets Please! (*10 minutes*) Each week begins with an activity option to involve children while others are being dropped off by parents.
- The *Welcome Time Activity* will excite children's interest and help them connect with the Bible Truth for the week.

All Aboard for Bible Truth! (*20 minutes*) Whole group, interactive Bible lessons invite students ages 6–11 to participate in the entire lesson. Whether it's role-playing characters in a Bible story or building walls out of milk cartons, kids will be engaged in exciting, hands-on lessons.
- Pre- and post-lesson discussion times encourage children to talk about their own life experiences and tie their knowledge to the week's Bible Truth.
- *Use the Clues!* Practice is an important part of learning. In the *Sharing God with Others* program, children assume the role of agents on a mission. Kids have fun investigating the lives of Bible-time and modern-day missionaries to discover *What makes a good missionary?*

For every new truth kids uncover, they will collect a Mission Passcard. In the weeks that follow, students are repeatedly challenged to remember the mission truth connected with each Passcard. These "memory hooks" help new information stick with kids for a long time to come.

Bible Memory Waypoint (*5 minutes*). Many missionaries must learn another language to communicate the truth of God's love in a way people can understand. In this program, your students will learn another language too. American Sign Language! Each week's verse is presented with 3 to 4 words from American Sign Language. These words are underlined. You can find the ASL signs for the underlined words for each lesson at these websites:

- http://commtechlab.msu.edu/sites/aslweb/browser.htm
- http://www.lifeprint.com

Prayer Station *(15 minutes).* Small group prayer time for children. Wow! What an idea! Children break into small groups of three to five with an adult helper—we call them StationMasters. Using reproducible instruction cards, adults guide children to share concerns, praise God, and practice the four activities of prayer: *praise, ask, confess, give thanks.*

(Optional) ***Snack Stop and Activities*** *(10 minutes).* Tied to the theme of the lesson, you have options for snacks and activities in which lesson truths are practiced and shared. Look for the throttle icon which shows the level of mess, energy, or noise required for the activity!

On the Fast Track! Reproducible take-home pages invite families to interact in and through fun activities and Bible memory.

Are you looking for an additional way to motivate young learners? *Discipleship Junction* includes an optional incentive program which rewards students for completing home activities. Children return a signed *Fast Track!* ticket and choose a prize from the treasure box. If you have a new student, you might welcome that child with the choice of a treasure too! Simply cover and decorate a large shoebox. Fill with inexpensive items such as you might find at a party store.

HOW TO GET STARTED

1. ***Begin by recruiting StationMasters***—adult helpers who will guide children through the process of praying in small groups. Each week you'll give the StationMasters a reproducible instruction card with the day's prayer theme and prayer suggestions to use with children in a small group. Don't have enough adult volunteers? How about recruiting middle- or high-schoolers to shepherd a group

2. ***Set up your room.*** You'll need a big area for your large-group Bible teaching time. You'll also need to identify spaces for each of your small prayer groups. Don't forget that rearranging chairs and tables, or moving groups to a hallway is always an option. And children are willing helpers!

3. ***Photocopy reproducibles*** (see Resources) to parents and a church-supported missionary family. Mail these two or three weeks before you begin your children's ministry program. Also copy *On the Fast Track!* pages for each child, and *StationMaster Cards* for each adult helper.

4. ***Contact a local, short-term missionary.*** For lesson 8, you will need to arrange with a local short-term missionary to visit your class and share the highlights of his or her work.

5. ***Prepare a set of Mission Passcards for each child*** (see Resources). Copy these cards onto cardstock or stiff paper. Fold on the dotted line and hole punch to make a 2-sided card. You might even draft a Station Master helper to add some color to the cards! *(Optional)*: After kids have been fingerprinted and photographed for their I.D. card the first week, you can laminate the card sets, or cover each card with clear sticky plastic or just add a strip of tape at the top punched edge. Kids will collect a new card each week to keep on a binder ring. Don't forget to make extra sets for new students who may join the class later.

6. ***Prepare the Mission Files.*** You'll need a multi-pocket file portfolio with at least 13 pockets. Each of the Mission Adventures (see Resources) should be copied onto a separate sheet of paper and placed inside the pocket file portfolio. Put the missions in number order, each in its own pocket.

7. Gather and prepare your materials, set out your snacks, and you are ready to roll. So . . . **FULL SPEED AHEAD! ALL ABOARD FOR DISCIPLESHIP JUNCTION!**

LESSON ONE:
What in the World are Missionaries?

Memory Verse:
Therefore <u>go</u> and make disciples of all nations, <u>baptizing</u> them in the name of the <u>Father</u> and of the <u>Son</u> and of the Holy Spirit (Matthew 28:19).

Bible Basis:
Mark 6:7–13

Bible Truth:
Missionaries are followers of Jesus who tell others about Him.

You Will Need:

- ☐ 13 Mission Adventure Files (see Resources, 97)
- ☐ Mission Files (file portfolio with at least 13 pockets)
- ☐ Bibles
- ☐ 1 poster board
- ☐ butcher paper
- ☐ sequins, small beads, buttons, glitter
- ☐ *On the Fast Track! #1* take-home paper
- ☐ *StationMaster Card #1*
- ☐ *(Optional)* treasure box
- ☐ *(Optional)* Snack: apple slices, animal crackers, napkins
- ☐ *(Optional)* Activity #1: camera, ink pad, wet wipes, hole punch, 1¹/₂" binder ring, copies of Mission Passcard #1, for each child (see Resources, 84)

 When you see this icon, it means preparation will take more than five minutes.

GET SET!
(Lesson Preparation)

- ■ 🌐 Copy the following questions and Bible references onto separate slips of paper:
  1. What is a missionary? Read John 20:21 and decide what it tells you.
  2. What is a missionary? Read Matthew 28:19 and decide what it tells you.
  3. What is a missionary? Read Acts 1:8 and decide what it tells you.
  4. What is a missionary? Read 2 Corinthians 5:18-20. What does verse 20 say we are?
  5. What is a missionary? Read Romans 10:13-15 and decide what it tells you.
- ■ Make a copy of the Mission Passcard #1 (I.D. card) on card stock for each child. Cut them out.
- ■ Make a copy of *On the Fast Track! #1* for each child.
- ■ Make a copy of *StationMaster Card #1* for each helper.
- ■ 🌐 Print this week's memory verse on the poster board.
- ■ Print "Missionary" on a length of butcher paper in large outline block letters. Hang it at the front of the classroom for the Welcome Time Activity.
- ■ 🌐 Make a separate copy of each of the 13 Mission Files (see Resources, 97) and file each one in number order in a pocket of the portfolio. You will use these throughout this program.
- ■ 🌐 After class, print the photos (1¹/₂" x 1") and attach to each child's I.D. card in the upper right corner. When new children come to class, a helper can be responsible for putting their photos and fingerprints on an I.D. card so all will have a complete set of Mission Passcards by week 13.

■ Make a copy of the missionary letter (see Resources, 98) and send it to a church-supported missionary family.

TICKETS PLEASE!
(Welcome and Bible Connection)

■ **Objective:** *To introduce the term "missionary"*

Welcome Time Activity: More Than a Word

Materials: butcher paper, markers, glue, sequins or small beads, tape
   As the children arrive, ask them to decorate the word "missionary" by coloring or gluing sequins and beads to the large letters.

Before beginning the class, send a helper with the Mission Files out of sight. When everyone has arrived, call the children to the lesson area. Build an atmosphere of excitement as you explain that you and the children are beginning a series of important missions together. These weekly missions will lead you to some new and important information. Signal the helper to hurry in urgently and hand you the Mission Files. The helper should say with drama: **You've been given a mission!**

Sharing Time and Bible Connection

   Introduce today's lesson with this large-group discussion. As you talk, give every child the opportunity to say something.
   Wow! A mission! Let's see what it is. Have you ever done something like this before? Let's see what we're supposed to do. Take out the Mission #1 sheet from the portfolio. Read it aloud. **Okay, here's our assignment. Today we must discover what the word "missionary" means.**

■ **What do you think a missionary is?** Collect children's input and help them arrive at this definition: A follower of Jesus who tells others about Him.

■ **Does anyone know a missionary?** Let students share their experiences and information.

■ **What does a missionary do?** (pray, tell others about Jesus, teach, care for others, etc.)

Help your students connect the discussion to the Bible passage from Mark 6:7-13. **God wants every single person on earth to know about Him. When Jesus was on earth, He taught His disciples how to tell everyone the Good News. The disciples were <u>missionaries who followed Jesus and told others about Him</u>.**

 ## ALL ABOARD FOR BIBLE TRUTH

Bible Discover and Learn Time

Mark 6:7-13

■ *Objective: Children will study Mark 6:7–13 to understand that Jesus taught his disciples how to tell others about God.*

■ *Materials: Bibles, pencils, "What is a Missionary?" question slips*

Divide the class into five groups (if you have a small class, make fewer groups, but give each group additional slips). Hand out pencils and a different verse reference to each group. Then assign groups a place to work.

Groups should first choose someone to be speaker. The speaker will read the question aloud. All group members will look up the verse and read it. As a group, children should decide how the verse answers the question. When all groups have finished, call them together. Ask each speaker to share what the group found.

Summarize all the answers: **God sent Jesus to bring us the message that God loves us and will forgive our sin. Now that Jesus is in heaven, God gives us this job of bringing the message to others. Many people at home and far away have never heard that Jesus died for them. It's our job to tell them.**

Those who go will make disciples. How do they do that? By telling people why Jesus died and how they can know Him. And people all over the world, in all

nations, need to hear that. Missionaries share God with people right around them in their neighborhoods and schools, and in faraway places, too. Another name for doing this is an ambassador. An ambassador is a person sent to give a message or do a job.

Now that you know better what the word missionary means, can you think of someone you know who does this? (Let children answer.) **Have you ever told someone who Jesus is, and that He wants to forgive their sins and give them life in heaven that never ends? If you have, YOU are a missionary too!**

Use the Clues!
(Bible Review)

Every week, we'll be given a new mission to do. And we'll make a set of Mission Passcards to help us keep track of our missions. Later today we'll make our first one—an I.D. card!

Let's see what you remember about today's mission. Use these review questions to check children's understanding:

■ **What is a missionary?** (<u>Missionaries are people who follow Jesus and tell others about Him</u>.)

■ **Where could a missionary go to tell others about Jesus?** (to any place in the world, but also to neighbors)

■ **Why does Jesus send people out as missionaries?** (some people don't know Him and need to hear that He loves them and died to forgive them their sins.)

BIBLE MEMORY WAYPOINT   Matthew 28:19
(Scripture Memory)

■ *Objective: Children will hide God's Word in their hearts for guidance, protection, and encouragement.*

Therefore <u>go</u> and make disciples of all nations, <u>baptizing</u> them in the name of the <u>Father</u> and of the <u>Son</u> and of the Holy Spirit (Matthew 28:19).

In this program, as you teach each week's verse you will also teach the American Sign Language sign for the underlined words. You can find these signs at these websites:

■ **http://commtechlab.msu.edu/sites/aslweb/browser.htm**

■ **http://www.lifeprint.com**

People speak different languages all over the world. How would a missionary talk to the people in Africa or Nepal? Let children respond. **Some missionaries must learn a new language to be able to share the truth of God's love in a way people can understand. We're also going to learn some words in a new language. This language is used by people who are deaf—American Sign Language.**

Demonstrate the signs for the underlined words as you say them. Repeat the verse phrase by phrase until students are familiar with the verse.

(Optional): If you choose, you can delegate this Bible memory section to a helper who will learn the ASL signs and teach them weekly.

PRAYER STATION

- **Objective:** *Children will explore and practice prayer for themselves in small groups.*
- **Materials:** *Copies of* StationMaster Card #1 *for each helper*

Break into small groups of three to five children. Assign a teen or adult helper to each small group and give each helper a copy of *StationMaster Card #1* (see Resources, 90) with ideas for group discussion and prayer.

SNACK STOP: TRAVEL ENERGY BUILDERS (Optional)

If you plan to provide a snack, this is an ideal time to serve it.

- **Materials:** *apple slices, animal crackers, napkins*

Hand out napkins and offer children apple slices and/or animal crackers. **Traveling can take lots of energy. In some places missionaries hike long trails. Crackers are easy to carry on a trip. Fruit gives you energy.**
Note: Always be aware of children with food allergies and have another option on hand if necessary.

APPLICATION

- **Objective:** *Children will have opportunities to show how the lesson works in their own lives through activities and take-home papers.*

Some children's ministries may allow children to play outside at this point. If yours does not, choose one of the following activities.

Mission I.D. Card

■ *Materials: copies of Mission Passcard #1 (I.D. card), ink pad, wet wipes, camera, pencils, binder rings, hole punch*

We recommend that you do this activity with your class so that every child has an I.D. card to use as a cover for a set of Mission Passcards. We've included an additional activity below in case you have extra time.

Today when missionaries go to foreign lands, they need a picture passport. This I.D. card will be your passport for travel. Then, each week you'll receive a Mission Passcard to collect on a binder ring with your I.D. card.

Help children roll their thumbs on the inkpad and then onto the back of their I.D. cards. Offer wet wipes to clean off the ink. StationMasters can help children fill in the form and sign their names at the bottom of the card. Then, hole punch the card and put a binder ring through it. Finally, photograph each child in front of a plain background, like a wall or door.

Note: After class you'll attach printed photos to ID cards where noted. You can laminate the cards or cover them with sticky plastic sheets if you wish.

Missionary Ship Shape Drill

Explain that missionaries often have to cope with hardships and it helps to be in good physical shape. To be prepared, they can do some exercises.

■ 1st drill: Run 'n' drop. Have the children run in place for 10-15 seconds, drop to the floor on their tummies, then jump to their feet again and run in place. Repeat several times.

■ 2nd drill: Jumping jacks. Do 10 jumping jacks together as you count.

■ 3rd drill: Sit 'n' stretch. Have children sit on the floor and stretch out arms, legs, and back together.

Be encouraging and allow children to do what they're able.

ON THE FAST TRACK! *(Take-Home Papers)*

(Optional) treasure box. Give each child an *On the Fast Track!* paper. **Each week you can take home an *On the Fast Track!* paper and do the activities and practice the memory verse. When you've done those things, ask an adult to sign the ticket (point it out). Bring back the ticket and you can visit the treasure box** (hold up box). **Now, who wants to take home an *On the Fast Track!* paper?** Get children excited about doing the weekly activities and receiving prizes.

LESSON TWO: Transformation

Paul • Adoniram Judson

Memory Verse:
Teaching them to <u>obey</u> everything I have <u>commanded</u> you. And surely I am with you <u>always</u>, to the very <u>end</u> of the age (Matthew 28:20).

Bible Basis:
Acts 9—28

Bible Truth:
God can turn unbelievers into missionaries.

You Will Need:

- [ ] push pins
- [ ] cardstock or stiff paper
- [ ] Mission Files
- [ ] Mission Passcard #2 (see Resources, 84)
- [ ] binder rings with I.D. cards from last week
- [ ] building blocks, shoe boxes, clean milk jugs, etc.
- [ ] 1 poster board
- [ ] classroom size world map you can write on
- [ ] *On the Fast Track! #2* take-home paper
- [ ] *StationMaster Card #2*
- [ ] *(Optional)* treasure box
- [ ] *(Optional)* Snack: coconut macaroons or coconut-covered doughnut holes
- [ ] *(Optional)* Activity #1: masking tape, five non-breakable items (empty soda bottles, rectangular blocks, plastic bowling pins) and one ball per team
- [ ] *(Optional)* Activity #2: several copies of bookmark pattern (see Resources, 88) on cardstock, scissors, felt or vinyl squares cut in thirds, holepunch, ribbon, markers or fabric paint

When you see this icon, it means preparation will take more than five minutes.

GET SET!
(Lesson Preparation)

- ▪ Make a copy of *On the Fast Track! #2* take-home paper for each child.
- ▪ Make a copy of *StationMaster Card #2* for each helper.
- ▪ Photocopy, fold, and hole punch a Mission Passcard #2 for each child on cardstock or stiff paper.
- ▪ Make a copy of "Paul's Story" and of "Adoniram's Story" in the All Aboard section. Ask two StationMasters to help with this part. Give each helper a story.
- ▪ Cut quarter-sized circles out of cardstock. Write the name "Paul" on one circle and "Adoniram Judson" on the other. Glue each circle to the head of a pushpin.
- ▪ Hang up the map of the world.
- ▪ Set out building blocks, shoe boxes, clean milk jugs, etc. for the Welcome Time Activity.
- ▪ If using Activity #2, make several copies of the bookmark pattern on cardstock.
- ▪ Arrange with a StationMaster helper to bring in the Mission Files with urgency and drama during the Sharing Time today and following weeks.
- ▪ Print this week's memory verse on the poster board.

TICKETS PLEASE!
(Welcome and Bible Connection)

- ▪ **Objective:** *To excite children's interest and connect how they interact with each other and God with the Bible Truth, children will construct a wall.*

Welcome Time Activity: Building Walls

■ *Materials:* *building blocks, shoe boxes, clean milk jugs, etc.*
As children arrive, direct them to the building materials. Ask them to build a wall as high and wide as they can. Encourage them to work on one big wall together instead of making a number of small walls. Leave the wall standing. When everyone has arrived, call the children to the lesson area.

Sharing Time and Bible Connection

Introduce today's lesson by discussing the following questions. Direct the children's attention to the wall built during the *Welcome Time Activity.* As you talk, give every child the opportunity to say something.

People build all sorts of walls. Some are made out of things people can see and some are made of things that people can't see.
■ **What kind of walls do people build that can't be seen?** (walls in their hearts against people or things they don't like)
■ **How do you think people build these invisible walls?** (they feel angry, jealous, afraid, or sorry for themselves)
■ **How do these walls affect our friendship with God?** (Walls make us take our eyes off of God and forget what He wants.)
■ **How can we ask God to break down our walls?** (prayer)

Signal the helper waiting outside to hurry in urgently and hand you the Mission Files. The helper should say with drama: **You've been given a mission!**
Say: **Wow! Another mission! Let's see what we're supposed to do today.** Ask a child to take out Mission #2 from the Mission Files. Read or let the child read it to your class. **To complete our mission today, we must investigate the lives of two people—Paul from the Bible and Adoniram Judson. We need to discover if <u>God can make missionaries out of unbelievers</u>.**

 # ALL ABOARD FOR BIBLE TRUTH   Acts 9—28

(Bible Discover and Learn Time)

■ **Objective:** *Children will study Paul's life in Acts 9—28 and hear about Adoniram Judson to learn that God can turn unbelievers into missionaries.*
■ **Materials:** *Copy of Paul and Adoniram Judson stories (below), world map, "Paul" and Adoniram" push pins, extra pins*

Today we're going to act out our Bible story with a freeze frame drama. Explain that when you pause a movie and it stays on one picture, this is a freeze frame. Divide the children into two groups. Have a StationMaster take the first group and a copy of Paul's story to one side of the room. You should take the second group and Adoniram's story to the other side. Help the groups decide how to show one of the freeze frames. Suggestions are presented in parentheses. Allow five minutes for groups to practice the four still scenes, then regather to perform for each other.

Paul's Story

#1: **This story takes place in Bible times after Jesus had died on the cross, came back to life, and then went to heaven. There was a man named Saul (Acts 13:9). He knew all about the Bible and was very smart. Saul did not believe Jesus was God. He hated Jesus' followers and traveled from city to city putting them in jail (Acts 26:9-11)** (Show Saul angry grabbing people to throw in jail.)

#2: **Saul and some other people were walking to the city of Damascus to put more Christians in jail (Acts 9:1-2). A bright, blinding light suddenly flashed around Saul and his friends. Saul fell to the ground (Acts 9:3-4).** (Show Saul on the ground with arms over his eyes, his friends shocked.)

#3 **A loud voice said, "Saul, why are you trying to hurt me?" Saul answered, "Who are you?" The voice replied, "I am Jesus who you are trying to hurt" (Acts 9:4-6). Jesus told Saul to get up and go into the city where he would be told what to do. But when he got up, he couldn't see. He was blind! His friends led him into the city (Acts 9:6-9).** (Show Saul groping around blindly as others lead him.)

#4: **Saul was blind for three days. Then God sent a man named Ananias to pray for him. God changed his name to Paul. He was filled with the Holy Spirit and had power to do God's work. And he could see again (Acts 9:10-19).** (Ananias prays for Paul, Paul prays, vision restored.) **Paul traveled all over to tell people, especially those who weren't Jews, about Jesus. <u>God made an unbeliever into a missionary</u>.** (Paul powerfully preaching, Paul traveling.)

Adoniram's Story

#1: **Adoniram Judson lived in the United States about 200 years ago. His family believed and followed God, but he didn't. When he went to college, Adoniram didn't want anything to do with God. He and his friends thought only of themselves.** (Show Adoniram partying with friends.)

#2: **When Adoniram returned home, his family tried to tell him why he should believe in Jesus. He got tired of listening and left to find his own adventures. Adoniram came to a town and needed a place to sleep. All the rooms at the inn were full, so the innkeeper said he must share a room with a sick man and hang up a blanket in between them. Adoniram was desperate, so he said yes.** (Show Adoniram and innkeeper talking, gesturing about sick man and blanket.)

#3: **The sick person moaned and groaned in pain all night. People came in to help him. Adoniram didn't get much sleep. Adoniram heard the poor man dying on the other side of the blanket. He imagined it was an old man.** (Adoniram sits up in his bed with hand cupped to his ear to hear what's happening to the sick man.)

#4: **The next morning Adoniram learned that the man had died. The innkeeper told him the dead man's name. It was one of his best friends from school! What a shock! Adoniram realized that he really did need to know God. So he went to school to learn the Bible and then traveled across the ocean to share Jesus with people who never heard of Him. He was a missionary in Burma. He put the Bible in their language of Burmese so they could read it. God used him to tell a lot of people about Jesus. <u>God made an unbeliever into a missionary</u>.** (Adoniram preaches to groups of people.)

Once groups are prepared, you or a helper will read the script as students perform the freeze frames. After groups have presented their freeze frames, summarize:

What do the lives of Paul and Adoniram have in common? (both lived their own way until God got their attention) **How did God change both people?** (<u>God made the unbelievers into missionaries.</u>)

Go to the wall map. **We'll keep track of all the missionaries we study. Paul was a missionary for God. He was born in a city named Tarsus.** Place "Paul" push pin in southern Turkey. **Where did Paul go?** The Bible says he went many places. Pick three places to place pins: Rome, Jerusalem, and Greece. Draw lines from Tarsus to each place. **Adoniram was born in the United States.** Place "Adoniram" pushpin in New England. **Where did he go?** Place another pin in Burma. Draw a line from New England to Burma. **Adoniram didn't go to as many places as Paul, but look at how far away from his home he went!**

Use the Clues!
(Bible Review)
■ *Materials: binder rings with I.D. card for each child, copies of Mission Passcard #2*

Ask helpers to hand out children's I.D. cards on rings. Hand out Mission Passcard #2 to each child. Briefly read through them together and help children place these cards on their rings behind their I.D. cards.

Use these review questions to check children's understanding of the lesson. Today, and in the weeks to follow, children may use their Mission Passcards to find answers.

Okay, Let's see what you remember.
■ **What is a missionary?** (a follower of Jesus who tells others about Him)
■ **What is the message of a missionary?** (God loves us, He has made a way for our sin to be forgiven through His son Jesus)
■ **How did Paul live before he knew God?** (he lived his own way, he wanted to get rid of people who followed Jesus)
■ **How did he become a follower of Christ?** (God got his attention with a bright light that blinded him, God talked to him and made him understand Jesus was really God.)
■ **How did Adoniram live before he knew God?** (he didn't care about God)
■ **How did he become a Christian?** (God got his attention when his best friend died one night right near him. Adoniram found out he needed to follow God.)
■ **What did Paul and Adoniram do after they became Christians?** (They both traveled to places where people needed to know Jesus, and spent their lives telling others about Him.)

Helpers should collect card sets for use next week.

BIBLE MEMORY WAYPOINT!

Matthew 28:20

(Scripture Memory)

- **Objective:** *Children will hide God's Word in their hearts for guidance, protection, and encouragement.*

Teaching them to <u>obey</u> everything I have <u>commanded</u> you. And surely I am with you always, to the very <u>end</u> of the <u>age</u> (Matthew 28:20).

As you teach today's Bible memory verse phrase by phrase, demonstrate the ASL motions for the underlined words and have children do the motions with you. You can learn the signs for these words at these websites:

- **http://commtechlab.msu.edu/sites/aslweb/browser.htm**
- **http://www.lifeprint.com**

If you choose, delegate the teaching of the memory verse to a helper who will learn the ASL signs and teach them weekly.

After learning today's verse, help the children recite last week's memory verse. Then put last week's and this week's verses together. You could choose to do this in small groups with StationMaster helpers in each group.

PRAYER STATION

- **Objective:** *Children will explore and practice prayer for themselves in small groups.*
- **Materials:** *Copies of* StationMaster Card #2 *for each helper*

Break into small groups of three to five children. Assign a teen or adult helper to each small group and give each helper a copy of *StationMaster Card #2* (see Resources, 91) with ideas for group discussion and prayer.

SNACK TIME: BURMESE COCONUT TREATS (Optional)

If you plan to provide a snack, this is an ideal time to serve it.

- **Materials:** *coconut macaroons or doughnut holes rolled in shredded coconut*

What country did Adoniram go to as a missionary? Burma. Now it's called Myanmar. Coconut is a common food there. You can try coconut in these cookies (doughnuts). People in Myanmar also use the milky liquid that's inside coconuts in their cooking. Talk to children about their experiences trying coconut and other exotic foods. *Note: Always be aware of children with food allergies and have another option on hand if necessary.*

APPLICATION

■ **Objective:** *Children will have opportunities to show how the lesson works in their own lives through activities and take-home papers.*

Some children's ministries may allow children to play outside at this point. If yours does not, choose one of the following activities.

Knock 'Em Down!

■ **Materials:** *five nonbreakable items (empty soda bottles, rectangular blocks, plastic bowling pins) and one ball per team, masking tape*

To get Paul's and Adoniram's attention, God had to knock them down. Let's play a game called "Knock 'em down!" Divide the class into teams. Give each team a ball and five items. Teams will set up their five items in a cluster, like bowling pins. Make a masking tape line. Teams stand behind the line and each person gets one chance to roll the ball and try to knock over their items. The team that knocks them all down first wins. Play again, adjusting the set up to make it harder or easier as needed.

Transformation Bookmark

■ **Materials:** *make several copies of bookmark pattern (see Resources, 88) on cardstock, scissors, felt or vinyl squares cut in thirds, holepunch, ribbon, markers or fabric paint*

Today we learned that God can completely turn peoples' lives around. Have children use the patterns to trace a bookmark onto felt or vinyl. Show them how to cut the fringe on the bottom. Punch a hole at the top with scissors or a holepunch. (Do this for the children.) Give each child an eight-inch length of ribbon to tie through the hole.

Have children write the words "Knowing God Changes Us!" on their bookmarks using washable markers on felt; use permanent markers or fabric paints on vinyl. Caution children about getting wet paint on their clothes. Set bookmarks aside to dry. Shirt paints will need 24 hours to completely dry; you may want to keep them until the next class.

ON THE FAST TRACK! *(Take-home Papers)*

(Optional) treasure box. **When you take your *On the Fast Track!* paper home, you can do the activities and learn the verse. Then ask an adult to sign the ticket. When you bring the ticket back next week, you'll get a prize from the treasure box!** Award trips to the treasure box for children who brought back a signed ticket. Hand out the *On the Fast Track!* papers and encourage children to do the work and learn the verse at home.

Distribute the take-home papers just before children leave, with bookmarks if they made them.

LESSON THREE: No Turning Back

Memory Verse:
He gives <u>strength</u> to the <u>weary</u> and increases the <u>power</u> of the <u>weak</u> (Isaiah 40:29).

Bible Basis:
Acts 16:16–36

Bible Truth:
God gives missionaries the strength to keep on in hard times.

Silas · Mary Slessor

You Will Need:

- [ ] pushpins
- [ ] 1 poster board and cardstock
- [ ] Mission Files
- [ ] Mission Passcard #3
- [ ] binder rings with Mission Passcard sets
- [ ] world map
- [ ] ball of yarn
- [ ] large sheets of paper
- [ ] soft balls
- [ ] *On the Fast Track! #3* papers
- [ ] *StationMaster Card #3*
- [ ] (Optional) treasure box
- [ ] (Optional) Snack: dried banana chips, fresh bananas
- [ ] (Optional) Activity #1: up to 15 soft foam balls, 10 to 15 large pieces of cardboard to be used as shields, masking tape
- [ ] (Optional) Activity #2: a large, multi-colored bead for each child, easy-bake polymer clay in bright colors, elastic beading thread, large toothpicks.

When you see this icon, it means preparation will take more than five minutes.

GET SET!
(Lesson Preparation)

- ■ Make a copy of *On the Fast Track! #3* paper for each child.
- ■ Make a copy of *StationMaster Card #3* for each helper.
- ■ Photocopy, fold, and hole punch Mission Passcard #3 for each child on cardstock or stiff paper.
- ■ Cut quarter-sized circles out of cardstock. Write the name "Silas" on one circle and "Mary Slessor" on the other. Glue each circle to the head of a pushpin.
- ■ For the Welcome Activity, draw three targets, each on a separate sheet of paper, and each with four concentric circles. On each outer circle print, "Extra chores." On each second circle print "Cannot play with friends." On each third circle print "I feel sick." In each bulls-eye print, "More homework!" Tape the targets to different walls.
- ■ Create a masking tape line to divide the room into two parts if using Activity #1. The line should divide the room unequally so that one section is three-fourths of the space.
- ■ Arrange with a StationMaster helper to bring in the Mission Files with urgency and drama during the Sharing Time today.
- ■ Print this week's memory verse on the poster board.

TICKETS PLEASE!
(Welcome and Bible Connection)

- ■ **Objective:** *To excite children's interest and connect with the Bible Truth, children will throw balls at targets.*

Welcome Time Activity: My Least Favorite Thing

◼ *Materials 3 large targets, tape, markers, 9 soft balls*
As the children arrive, direct them toward one of the targets so that each target has an equal number of students. Assign a helper at each target to facilitate. Each child chooses their least favorite thing on the target and has three tries to hit that circle. Helpers should lead groups in cheering as they watch. When everyone has arrived, call the children to the lesson area.

Sharing Time and Bible Connection

Introduce today's lesson by discussing the following questions. As you talk, give every child the opportunity to say something.

◼ **What's something you really don't like to do?**
◼ **How do you try to get out of doing that thing?**
◼ **Do you think God would ever ask you to do something you didn't want to do?**

Signal the helper waiting outside to hurry in urgently and hand you the Mission Files. The helper should say with drama: **You've been given a mission!**

Say: **Wow! Another mission! Let's see what our assignment is for today.** Choose a child to take out Mission #3 from the Mission Files and read it aloud. **To complete our mission today, we need to study the lives of two people—Silas and Mary Slessor. I wonder who they are. Our mission is to discover where <u>missionaries find strength to keep on during hard times</u>. How can they obey God when things get really hard?**

ALL ABOARD FOR BIBLE TRUTH   Acts 16:16–36
(Bible Discover and Learn Time)

◼ *Objective: Children will study Acts 16:16–36 to discover God gives missionaries strength in hard times.*
◼ *Materials: Large ball of yarn, scissors, world map, markers, "Silas" and "Mary" pushpins, extra pins*

Arrange children in a loose circle. **Do you remember Paul from last week?** Let children respond. **Paul's friend, Silas, was also a missionary. Paul and Silas traveled from city to city telling people about Jesus. But when they got to a city called Philippi, there was big trouble.**

Paul had commanded a demon to leave a servant girl, and the people of the town got really mad at them. A crowd came to attack them. How would you feel?

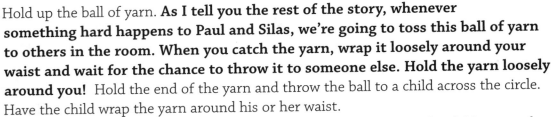

Hold up the ball of yarn. **As I tell you the rest of the story, whenever something hard happens to Paul and Silas, we're going to toss this ball of yarn to others in the room. When you catch the yarn, wrap it loosely around your waist and wait for the chance to throw it to someone else. Hold the yarn loosely around you!** Hold the end of the yarn and throw the ball to a child across the circle. Have the child wrap the yarn around his or her waist.

An angry crowd was ready to attack the missionaries! Direct the child to toss the yarn to someone across the room, holding the yarn at the waist. Repeat this whenever you see "toss" in parentheses. **The town leaders commanded that soldiers would tear the clothes off Paul and Silas.** (Toss.) **Then Silas was beaten!** (Toss.) **After both Silas and Paul were beaten up, they were locked into a prison.** (Toss.) **How do you think they felt then?**

The city leaders ordered the jailkeeper to watch them carefully. So he locked them in the inside cell. It was probably very dark and stinky. (Toss.) **To make sure Silas and Paul wouldn't try to escape, the jailer put their feet in stocks.** Explain this would be like putting their feet in handcuffs. (Toss.)

All day and night they stayed in that dark jail. But Paul and Silas prayed and sang songs to God. Suddenly, at midnight, there was a great earthquake! (Toss.) **The prison doors flew open, and the prisoner's chains fell off! They could all escape! The jailor was so upset, he was ready to kill himself. But Paul yelled, "Don't hurt yourself. We're all here!" Paul and Silas could have escaped, but they stayed!**

The jailer took Paul and Silas to his own house, cleaned their cuts, and gave them food. Silas told him about Jesus, and the jailer's whole family decided to follow Jesus. They all became Christians because Paul and Silas had stayed where God wanted them.

Explain that the yarn tossing will continue with this next story about another missionary.

Our second story is about a woman named Mary Slessor. She grew up in Scotland about 150 years ago. She went to Nigeria to tell people about God. She cared for people there and even helped a tribal chief get well from a serious sickness.

One day, Mary got a message that two tribes were ready to go to war with each other. Mary didn't want them to fight, so she decided to walk to their villages to stop them. Her friends asked her not to go. It was night; walking was dangerous. (Toss.) **There were hungry animals.** (Toss.) **But Mary was determined to go, so she went with two men to carry her lanterns. Mary walked all night.** (Toss.)

In the morning when she arrived, the warriors were getting ready to attack each other. (Toss.) **Mary was so tired that she could barely walk.** (Toss.) **Yet she ran into the middle of the battlefield and yelled at them to stop.** (Toss.) **She told them to settle their argument in a peaceful way.**

One of the chiefs stepped forward and said, "We're glad you came. This is a mistake. We don't want anyone to die." The chief who spoke was the same chief that she had helped get well. Because Mary had served them, the chief was willing to listen to her. A big battle was stopped and no one died that day. These tribes had a new chance to hear about Jesus. Let those without yarn wrap the ball around their waists. Everyone should be trapped within the strings of yarn around them.

Hard times feel like you're trapped, kind of like you're caught in the yarn. As you talk, take out the scissors and carefully cut the yarn off. **Did God keep the missionaries in**

our stories from hard times? No. He let the hard times happen, but God made good things come from those hard times. Silas and Paul helped the jailer and his family became Christians. Mary served the tribes and the warriors listened to her. God gives missionaries the strength to not give up in the middle of hard times. If God allows you to be in the middle of something difficult, don't turn back. Follow Him and do what He says. <u>God gives missionaries the strength to keep on even in hard times.</u>

The Bible first mentions Silas in Jerusalem (Acts 15:22). Place the "Silas" pushpin in Jerusalem. **Where did Silas go?** Stick a pushpin in Philippi, which is in northern Greece. Draw a line between the pins. **Mary was born in Scotland.** Place the "Mary" pushpin in Scotland. **Where did Mary go to serve God?** Place another pin on Nigeria. Draw a line.

Use the Clues!
(Bible Review)

■ *Materials: binder rings with Mission Passcard rings, Mission Passcard #3*

Ask helpers to hand out Mission Passcard rings. Give Mission Passcard #3 to each child. Briefly read them together and help children place these cards on their rings behind their I.D. cards.

Use these review questions to check children's understanding of the lesson. Today, and in the weeks to follow, children may use their Mission Passcards to find answers.

Okay, let's see what you remember.

■ **What kind of man was Silas?** (he didn't give up when things were hard)

■ **What did Silas do in prison?** (he prayed and sang worship songs, he didn't give up)

■ **What happened because Silas trusted God,** **even in prison?** (God gave him the chance to tell the jailer and his family about Jesus)

■ **What kind of woman was Mary?** (she lived with tribal people in Nigeria, she cared for the chief when he was sick; she was willing to walk all night to stop people from fighting, she was brave)

■ **What happened because Mary stayed where things were hard?** (the tribal men didn't hurt or kill each other, more people were willing to listen to God's message of peace)

If time allows, review previous lessons with a game. Divide class into two teams, A and B. Ask several questions based on the Mission Passcards from previous lessons. Address questions alternately to Team A, then B and let them decide on a group answer. Winning team has the most correct answers.

Helpers should collect card sets for use next week.

BIBLE MEMORY WAYPOINT
(Scripture Memory)

Isaiah 40:29

■ **Objective:** *Children will hide God's Word in their hearts for guidance, protection, and encouragement.*

He gives <u>strength</u> to the <u>weary</u> and increases the <u>power</u> of the <u>weak</u> (Isaiah 40:29).

As you teach today's Bible memory verse phrase by phrase, demonstrate the ASL motions for the underlined words and have children do the motions with you. You can learn the signs for these words at these websites:

- http://commtechlab.msu.edu/sites/aslweb/browser.htm
- http://www.lifeprint.com

If you choose, delegate the teaching of the memory verse to a helper who will learn the ASL signs and teach them weekly. Have students give each other high 5's for learning the verse.

PRAYER STATION

- *Objective: Children will explore and practice prayer for themselves in small groups.*
- *Materials: Copies of* StationMaster Card # 3 *for each helper*

Break into small groups of three to five children. Assign a teen or adult helper to each small group and give each helper a copy of *StationMaster Card #3* (see Resources, 91) with ideas for group discussion and prayer.

SNACK STOP: NIGERIAN BANANA BITS (Optional)

If you plan to provide a snack, this is an ideal time to serve it.

- *Materials: dried banana chips, fresh bananas cut in halves or thirds*

People in Nigeria eat many different foods than we do, and use different ways to prepare food. Cooking bananas are used, but they don't taste sweet like the bananas we're used to. Offer the banana chips and fresh bananas.
Note: Always be aware of children with food allergies and have another option on hand if necessary.

APPLICATION

■ **Objective:** *Children will have opportunities to show how the lesson works in their own lives through activities and take-home papers.*

Some children's ministries may allow children to play outside at this point. If yours does not, choose one of the following activities.

 Shield of Protection!

■ **Materials:** *2' x 2' sheets of cardboard for shields, soft foam balls, masking tape*

Tape a line down the middle of the room, then divide the class into two equal groups. Give shields to one group, and balls to the other. (If your class is large, kids may share a shield.) Each group must stay on their side of the masking tape. **Sometimes when we're having hard times, it feels like things are hitting us. But if you know Jesus, you have His protection, like a shield.**

    Explain that the ball-throwers will stay on one side of the taped line and try to hit the players with the shields. Children will dodge the balls or use shields to block the balls thrown at them. When players are hit, they must leave the game and wait on the sidelines. Helpers can help roll back balls that have been tossed. When everyone has been hit let the teams switch sides. At the end, explain that when God is our Shield, we are safe in Him, even during difficult times.

 Nigerian Beads

■ **Materials:** *a large multi-colored bead for each child, polymer clay in assorted bright colors, elastic thread, large toothpicks*

Explain that the Nigerian people make beautiful sculptures, fabrics, pottery, and beaded necklaces. Let each child choose one multi-colored bead as the centerpiece of their project. Give children wads of polymer clay in their choice of colors and have them sculpt additional beads. Make holes in the center of the beads with a toothpick and string them on elastic bead thread. Helpers can help tie the ends of the thread to secure the beads. Set aside to harden until the end of class. The string of beads can be worn as a bracelet or anklet.

 ## ON THE FAST TRACK! *(Take-home Papers)*

(Optional) treasure box. Award trips to the treasure box for children who brought back a signed *Fast Track!* ticket. **When you take your *On the Fast Track!* paper home, you can do the activities and learn the verse. Then ask a parent to sign the ticket. When you bring the ticket back next week, you'll get a prize from the treasure box.**

    Hand out the take-home papers just before children leave, with their Nigerian bead crafts if they made them.

Memory Verse:

<u>Two</u> are better than <u>one</u>, because they have a good <u>return</u> for their <u>work</u> (Ecclesiastes 4:9).

Bible Truth:

Missionaries work together to get the job done.

Bible Basis:

Acts 16:1–4; Romans 16:21; 1 Corinthians 4:17; 2 Corinthians 1:1; 1 Thessalonians 3:1–4; and 1 Timothy 1:3–4

You Will Need:

- ☐ pushpins
- ☐ cardstock or stiff paper
- ☐ Mission Files
- ☐ Mission Passcard #4
- ☐ Binder rings with Mission Passcard sets
- ☐ world map
- ☐ blindfolds
- ☐ plastic flying disc
- ☐ 3 sheets of poster board or large pieces of blank cardboard
- ☐ *On the Fast Track! #4*
- ☐ *StationMaster Card #4*
- ☐ (Optional) treasure box
- ☐ (Optional) Snack: canned chickpeas (garbanzo beans) in a serving bowl OR chickpea hummus with pita bread or tortilla chips, spoons or toothpicks
- ☐ (Optional) Activity #1: bag of mini-marshmallows; toothpicks
- ☐ (Optional) Activity #2: half sheets of white paper, dish detergent, shallow pans, two colors of acrylic paint, newspaper to cover table, paper towels

When you see this icon, it means preparation will take more than five minutes.

GET SET!
(Lesson Preparation)

- ■ Make a copy of *On the Fast Track! #4* for each child.
- ■ Make a copy of *StationMaster #4* for each helper.
- ■ Photocopy, fold, and hole punch Mission Passcard #4 for each child on cardstock or stiff paper.
- ■ Cut quarter-sized circles out of cardstock. Write the name "Timothy" on one circle and "Cook" on the other. Glue each circle to the head of a pushpin.
- ■ Write "Timothy" in large decorative writing that takes up most of one sheet of poster board, and cut into lots of puzzle pieces. Do the same with "Cook International" on the second poster board. Place each set of puzzle pieces in a box or bag.
- ■ Set up an obstacle course that 2 to 3 pairs of kids can navigate simultaneously, for the Welcome Activity.
- ■ Arrange with a StationMaster helper ahead of time to bring in the Mission Files with urgency and drama during the Sharing Time today.
- ■ Print this week's memory verse on the poster board.

TICKETS PLEASE!
(Welcome and Bible Connection)

- ■ **Objective:** *To excite children's interest and connect with Bible Truth that they may need to work with others, children will run an obstacle course.*

other made the puzzles come together faster than if each child had worked alone.

Timothy's life and Cook's ministry show us that <u>missionaries can work together to get the job done</u>.

Timothy was a missionary who helped Paul. The Bible first tells about him in a place called Lystra. Today that's called Turkey. Place the "Timothy" pushpin in central Turkey. **Where did Timothy go?** Stick another pushpin in Rome, Corinth (southern Greece), Thessalonica (northern Greece), and Ephesus (western Turkey). Draw lines from Lystra to each of these places.

Cook Communications Ministries International helps missionaries by giving books and telling people how to make books. They're in Colorado in the United States. Place the "Cook" pushpin in Colorado. **Where has Cook helped? They've helped missionaries all over the world. We'll mark two of those places.** Place pushpins in China and Iraq. Draw lines from Colorado Springs to each of those places.

Use the Clues!
(Bible Review)
- ***Materials:*** *Mission Passcard sets, copies of Mission Passcard #4*

Ask helpers to hand out children's I.D. cards on rings. Hand out Mission Passcard #4 to each child. Briefly read through them together and help children place these cards on their rings behind their I.D. cards. To make this review fun, play "Popcorn." Children sit on the floor as you ask a question. The first one to pop up gets a try at answering. If they can't answer correctly let another child pop up to help them. Allow kids to use their cards to help them answer.

Let's see what you remember:
- **What two missionaries worked together in** the New Testament? (Timothy and Paul)
- **How did Timothy help Paul?** (he went wherever Paul needed him to go, he could travel when Paul had to stay somewhere else, he taught and told about Jesus, was the pastor of a church)
- **How does a group like Cook Communications Ministries International help missionaries?** (they help people in other countries make books that tell about God's love, send books, help Bible clubs)
- **How has Cook done the work of a missionary?** (they send Bibles and books about God to places where there aren't any books, they help pastors and teachers teach others about Jesus)

After the game, have helpers collect the card rings.

BIBLE MEMORY WAYPOINT   Ecclesiastes 4:9

- ***Objective:*** *Children will hide God's Word in their hearts for guidance, protection, and encouragement.*

<u>Two</u> are better than <u>one,</u> because they have a good <u>return</u> for their <u>work</u> (Ecclesiastes 4:9).

As you teach today's Bible memory verse phrase by phrase, demonstrate the ASL motions for the underlined words and have children do the motions with you. You can learn the signs for these words at these websites:

- ■ http://commtechlab.msu.edu/sites/aslweb/browser.htm
- ■ http://www.lifeprint.com

If you choose, delegate the teaching of the memory verse to a helper who will learn the ASL signs and teach them weekly. When children are familiar with the verse, let them choose a partner and stand together as they learn the verse, to reinforce that "two are better than one."

PRAYER STATION

- ■ *Objective:* Children will explore and practice prayer for themselves in small groups.
- ■ *Materials:* Copies of StationMaster Card #4 for each helper

Break into small groups of three to five children. Assign a teen or adult helper to each small group and give each helper a copy of *StationMaster Card #4* (see Resources , 92) with ideas for group discussion and prayer.

SNACK STOP: IRAQI SNACK

If you plan to provide a snack, this is an ideal time to serve it.

- ■ *Materials:* canned chickpeas (garbanzo beans) in a serving bowl OR chickpea hummus with pita bread or tortilla chips, spoons or toothpicks

Do you remember the name of the city where Cook sends *Picture New Testaments*? It's Baghdad, in Iraq. One of the foods that children and adults eat often in Baghdad are chickpeas. They're also called garbanzo beans. Show the children the can of chickpeas and then the snack you've chosen. Let those who choose to taste the chickpeas. They can scoop the hummus with tortilla chips. Those who choose not to try the chickpeas or hummus can eat chips.

Note: Always be aware of children with food allergies and have another option on hand if necessary.

APPLICATION

■ *Objective: Children will have opportunities to show how the lesson works in their own lives through activities and take-home papers.*

Some children's ministries may allow children to play outside at this point. If yours does not, choose one of the following activities.

Give Your Support Challenge

■ **Materials:** *miniature marshmallows; toothpicks*

Let children work in small, multi-age teams of 3 or 4. Give each team a handful of marshmallows and about 20 toothpicks. Instruct them to use marshmallows to join toothpicks together into shapes that can stand alone. **This is a contest to see which group can build the strongest tower that can stand on its own and can hold up the weight of a book.** Give them a set amount of time, and then stop the activity. Give praise to groups with the highest tower, with the best cooperation, with the tower that can hold up the most weight, etc. Remind children that when missionaries work together, they can do more.

Marbled Paper

■ **Materials:** *half sheets of white paper, shallow pans, margarine tubs, two colors of acrylic paint, liquid fabric starch, paper towels, measuring cup and spoons, straw, newspaper to cover table*

In Middle Eastern countries like Iraq, arts like marbled paper are common. Making marbled papers is fun and easy! Set up several stations with an adult helper at each one:
■ Mix 1 Tbsp. acrylic paint with 2 Tbsp. water in a margarine tub. Repeat for second color. Set aside.
■ Put 1 cup of liquid fabric starch in a flat pan. Gently drop some of the paint mixture onto the surface of the liquid starch, drop by drop. Repeat with second color. Then swirl colors together a little with a straw or stir stick.
■ Gently lay a sheet of paper on top of the colors and lift carefully. Paint will adhere. Set aside to dry on newspapers. Repeat with more colors until every child has made a marbled paper. When papers are dry, children make take them home and write today's Bible verse on them.

ON THE FAST TRACK! *(Take-home Papers)*

(Optional) treasure box. Award trips to the treasure box for children who brought back a signed *Fast Track!* ticket. **When you take your *On the Fast Track!* paper home, you can do the activities and learn the verse. Then ask a parent to sign the *Fast Track!* ticket. When you bring the ticket back next week, you can choose a prize from the treasure box.** Hand out the take-home papers just before children leave, with their marbled papers if they made them.

LESSON FIVE: On the Home Front

Stephen • George Mueller

Memory Verse:

Dear <u>children</u>, let us not <u>love</u> with words or <u>tongue</u> but with actions and in truth (1 John 3:18).

Bible Basis:

Acts 6:1–10

Bible Truth:

Missionaries tell people about God wherever they live.

You Will Need:

- [ ] pushpins
- [ ] cardstock or stiff paper
- [ ] 1 poster board
- [ ] Mission Files
- [ ] Mission Passcard #5
- [ ] binder rings with Mission Passcard sets
- [ ] world map
- [ ] playdough
- [ ] 2 large (1½' x 5') pieces of butcher paper
- [ ] 2 half-sheets of paper per child
- [ ] *On the Fast Track!* #5
- [ ] *StationMaster Card #5*
- [ ] *(Optional)* treasure box
- [ ] *(Optional)* Snack: small baking powder biscuits or scones, jam, fruit flavored sweetened iced tea, plastic spoons, cups
- [ ] *(Optional)* Activity #2: square white paper, colored tissue paper, scissors, glue sticks

 When you see this icon, it means preparation will take more than five minutes.

GET SET!
(Lesson Preparation)

- Make a copy of *On the Fast Track!* #5 take-home paper for each child.
- Make a copy of *StationMaster Card #5* for each helper.
- Photocopy, fold, and hole punch Mission Passcard #5 for each child on cardstock or stiff paper.
- ⏱ Cut quarter-sized circles out of cardstock. Write the name "Stephen" on one circle and "George Mueller" on the other. Glue each circle to the head of a pushpin.
- On a large sheet of paper or a piece of poster board, print "Stephen" on one half and "George Mueller" on the other. Hang the sheet near your story area.
- Arrange with a StationMaster helper to rush in the Mission Files with urgency and drama during the Sharing Time today.
- ⏱ Print this week's memory verse on the poster board.

Play Dough Recipe

- 2 c. flour
- 1 c. salt
- 4 T. cream of tartar
- 1 pkg. unsweetened dry drink mix for scent and color
- 2 c. warm water
- 2 T. cooking oil

Stir over medium heat until mixture pulls away from sides to form a ball. Store in airtight container. *(for 8 to 10 children)*

TICKETS PLEASE!
(Welcome and Bible Connection)

■ **Objective:** *To excite children's interest and connect their neighborhoods and communities with the Bible Truth, children will mold their neighborhood using playdough.*

Welcome Time Activity: Welcome to My Neighborhood

■ **Materials:** *play dough*

As children arrive, direct them to the table and invite them to mold play dough houses or apartments and people to create a their neighborhood. Helpers should assist as needed and suggest that God cares about every person in their neighborhood as much as He does about the children in class. When everyone has arrived, call the children to the lesson area.

Sharing Time and Bible Connection

Introduce today's lesson with this interactive activity and discussion. As you talk, give every child the opportunity to say something. Use a white board or mount a large sheet of paper on an easel or wall next to you. Have assorted color markers at hand.

Let's create a neighborhood on this board/paper. Ask for volunteers to start drawing elements such as houses or apartments, trees, pets, cards, and other things that make up a neighborhood or community. Give each child a chance to draw one item; two children can work simultaneously for time's sake. As children draw, engage those watching in discussion.

■ **What does it take to make a neighborhood?**
■ **What kinds of people (old, young, different cultures, different economic levels) live in your neighborhood?**
■ **Do you think all the people who live in your neighborhood know Jesus as their own Savior?**
■ **Do you think a missionary might spend time around your neighborhood to share Jesus?**

After discussion time, help your students connect their discussion to the Bible story they are about to hear from Acts 6:1-10. Signal the helper waiting outside to hurry in urgently and hand you the Mission Files. The helper should say with drama: **You've been given a mission!** Say: **Wow! Another mission! Let's see what we're supposed to do today.** Ask a child to take out Mission #5 from the Mission Files. Read or let the child read it to your class. **To complete our mission today, we need to study the lives of two people—Stephen and George Mueller. We will find <u>where missionaries are working</u>.**

ALL ABOARD FOR BIBLE TRUTH   Acts 6:1-10
(Bible Discover and Learn Time)

■ **Objective:** *Children will study Acts 6:1-10 to learn about Stephen and George Mueller and find out that missionaries can tell people in their own cities and communities about God.*

■ **Materials:** *2 half-sheets of paper per child, markers or crayons, scissors, glue, 2 large (1½' x 5') pieces of butcher paper, tape*

Hand a half-sheet of paper to each child. **As you hear the story about a New Testament man named Stephen, imagine someone who Stephen might have helped. Draw a picture of that person and cut it out.** Wait for everyone to be settled before beginning the story.

After Jesus died, rose again, and went back to heaven, the disciples told everybody around them what Jesus had done. A lot of people trusted in Jesus as their Savior. These new followers of Jesus helped and cared for each other. They shared their food and belongings and were almost like a family together.

As more and more new believers of Jesus joined this "family," sometimes there were problems. Some of them thought they weren't getting as much food as others.

The disciples, who were Jesus' first friends while He was on earth, knew they needed help to solve the problem. Their main job was to let others know about Jesus. So they chose seven other men to help give out the food. One of these was Stephen.

It says in Acts that Stephen was full of faith and the Holy Spirit. Because Stephen went right to work serving the new Christians, the disciples could keep preaching to others. So this group of believers kept growing.

Stephen also did some miracles that the Holy Spirit gave him power to do. This helped new Christians see that God was leading them. Stephen's wisdom and faith in God helped people trust in God more. He was also a great teacher, but he chose to serve the people that lived around him. He saw that it was important to do the work God had given him. So what kinds of people did you imagine he helped? Let children show their drawings to the class. Helpers can oversee as children glue their drawings to the "Stephen" section of the butcher paper.

Hand out a second half-sheet of paper to each child.

Now as you hear about George Mueller, imagine someone George might have helped. Draw one picture of that person and cut it out.

George Mueller was born in a place called Prussia about 200 years ago. While he was in college, he decided to become a missionary. First he tried to become a missionary in Romania, but that didn't work out. Then, while he was in school in London, he decided to become a missionary to Jewish people. He could preach about Jesus to the Jews who lived around him. And this he did.

As George was teaching, he began to notice how many other people came to hear the message about God. George remembered that God's plan is for every single person to know about Jesus.

So George became a pastor and shared the good news about Jesus with people in England. Then a bad disease called cholera made hundreds of people get sick and die. George saw many little children without mothers or fathers. They had no one to take care of them. God gave George the idea to help these homeless children.

For the next 63 years, he took care of over 10,000 homeless children. George had thought that he was going to be a missionary in some far off place. But God had a different idea. Because George Mueller listened to God, thousands of children right in George's own city were raised with love.

Ask children to show their drawings of people George helped. Helpers can work with the children to glue their drawings on the butcher paper labeled "George."

What do Stephen's and George's lives show us? __Missionaries can tell people__ __about God wherever they live__. Point out that the paths are somewhat similar (i.e., both trusted God, both remained in the countries/cities where they were living, and God used them both in powerful ways) even though specifics were different.

Stephen was a missionary, but he didn't go to a far off land. He was part of the church of Jerusalem. Place the "Stephen" pushpin in Jerusalem. **Where did Stephen go?** Draw a circle around that tack.

George Mueller was also a missionary who stayed in his own country. God used him in England where he was living to take care of thousands of children. Place the "George'" pushpin in England. **Where did George go?** Draw a circle around that tack.

Use the Clues!
(Bible Review)
- *Materials:* *Mission Passcard rings, copies of Mission Passcard #5*

Have helpers hand out Mission Passcard rings. Then hand out Mission Passcard #5 which children will place on their rings behind card #4. Create two or more teams for the review. Ask a question about today's lesson or previous lessons. Choose a team to answer. If they answer wrong, ask another team. Rotate through the teams, so all have an equal chance to answer.

- **Who was Stephen?** (a believer in Bible times who was full of the Holy Spirit and served God)
- **How did God use Stephen?** (God used Stephen to take care of the people in the city, dividing up the food they shared, doing miracles and telling them about Jesus)
- **Who did George Mueller want to share God with?** (Jewish people first, then even non-Jewish people)
- **How did God use George Mueller?** (God used George to take care of orphans and tell a lot of people about Jesus in his own country) *Have helpers collect the card rings.*

BIBLE MEMORY WAYPOINT   1 John 3:18

■ **Objective:** *Children will hide God's Word in their hearts for guidance, protection, and encouragement.*

Dear <u>children</u>, let us not <u>love</u> with words or <u>tongue</u> but with actions and in truth (1 John 3:18).

As you teach today's Bible memory verse phrase by phrase, demonstrate the ASL motions and have children do the motions with you. You can learn the signs for these words at these websites:

■ **http://commtechlab.msu.edu/sites/aslweb/browser.htm**
■ **http://www.lifeprint.com**

If you choose, delegate the teaching of the memory verse to a helper who will learn the ASL signs and teach them weekly.

Teach your students the verse with the actions below. If you want to make it more interesting, divide into two groups, such as boys and girls. Have helpers work with each group to practice the verse with the signs. After a few minutes, let girls and boys demonstrate their learning.

PRAYER STATION

■ **Objective:** *Children will explore and practice prayer for themselves in small groups.*
■ **Materials:** *Copies of* StationMaster Card #5 *for each helper*

Break into small groups of three to five children. Assign a teen or adult helper to each small group and give each helper a copy of *StationMaster Card #5* (see Resources, 92) with ideas for group discussion and prayer.

SNACK STOP: BRITISH TEA TIME (Optional)

If you plan to provide a snack, this is an ideal time to serve it.
■ **Materials:** *small baking powder biscuits or scones, jam, fruit-flavored sweetened iced tea, plastic spoons, cups*

What country did George Mueller live in? (England). **A fun tradition in England is tea time, in the afternoon.** Serve the children a biscuit or scone and let them add a dollop of jam. Explain that the English drink hot tea, but they can have the fruity sweet iced tea.

Note: Always be aware of children with food allergies and have another option if necessary.

APPLICATION

■ *Objective: Children will have opportunities to show how the lesson works in their own lives through activities and take-home papers.*

Some children's ministries may allow children to play outside at this point. If yours does not, choose one of the following activities.

 Dragon's Tail Tag

Explain that this is a game children can play with others in their neighborhood. **Games like this help you build friendships, so you can tell your friends about Jesus.** Show boundaries, if any, for the game. Choose two children to be heads of the two dragons. (For a small class or small room, start with one dragon.) The others are free until they're tagged by the dragon head. Once tagged, children create the body and tail of the dragon by holding onto the shoulders of the last person on the dragon. Anyone attached to the dragon can tag free players. Eventually all the free players will be tagged.

 Window Pictures

■ *Materials: square white paper, colored tissue paper, scissors, glue sticks.*

People created decorative paper designs like these in the 1800s to put in their windows that didn't have curtains. Fold the square white paper into a triangle by folding one corner over to the opposite corner. Then fold again the opposite way to create a smaller triangle. Fold one more time to create a smaller triangle. Cut rounded or straight geometric designs on the two folded edges, similar to making a paper snowflake. Open up the fold and glue various colored tissue pieces over the cut-outs. Children can tape their window pictures onto a window at home.

 ON THE FAST TRACK! *(Take-home Papers)*

(Optional) treasure box. Award trips to the treasure box for children who brought back a signed ticket. Hand out the *On the Fast Track!* papers and encourage children to do the work and learn the verse at home. **When you take your *On the Fast Track!* paper home, you can do the activities and learn the verse. Then ask a parent to sign the ticket. When you bring the ticket back next week, you'll get a prize from the treasure box.**

Before they leave, give children their window pictures if they made them.

Barnabas • Betty Greene

Memory Verse:

The L ORD your God is with you, he is **mighty** to save. He will take great delight in you, he will quiet you with his love, he will rejoice over you with singing (Zephaniah 3:17).
Early elementary verse in *bold* type.

Bible Basis:
Acts 4:36–37;
9:26–28; 12:25—15:41

Bible Truth:
God loves to encourage His missionaries.

You Will Need:

- [ ] pushpins
- [ ] cardstock or stiff paper
- [ ] 1 poster board
- [ ] Mission Files
- [ ] Mission Passcard #6
- [ ] binder rings with Mission Passcard sets
- [ ] world map
- [ ] 2 uninflated balloons for each child
- [ ] 4" x 10" strips of paper
- [ ] 18 smooth rocks
- [ ] *On the Fast Track! #6* take-homes
- [ ] *StationMaster Card #6*
- [ ] *(Optional)* treasure box
- [ ] *(Optional)* Snack: bananas, raisins, small cups, spoons, knife
- [ ] *(Optional)* Activity #1: Barnabas and Betty balloons from the All Aboard section, stopwatch or clock with a second hand
- [ ] *(Optional)* Activity #2: paper towels, string, water, blue food coloring, bowls, old towels or cookie cooling racks

When you see this icon, it means preparation will take more than five minutes.

GET SET!
(Lesson Preparation)

- ■ Make a copy of *On the Fast Track! #6* papers for each child.
- ■ Make a copy of *StationMaster Card #6* for each helper.
- ■ Photocopy, fold, and hole punch Mission Passcard #6 on cardstock or stiff paper for each child
- ■ ⊕ Cut quarter-sized circles out of cardstock. Write the name "Barnabas" on one circle and "Betty Greene" on the other. Glue each circle to the head of a pushpin.
- ■ Set out the markers, crayons, and scissors, so that they are easily accessible to the children, and place the glue close to the large pieces of butcher paper.
- ■ Write "Barnabas" in permanent marker on half of the balloons and "Betty" on the other half.
- ■ ⊕ Write one word of the memory verse on each of the rocks. Do not write the words that are underlined. Write repeated words only once.
- ■ Arrange with a StationMaster helper to bring in the Mission Files with urgency and drama during the Sharing Time today and following weeks.
- ■ ⊕ Print this week's memory verse on the poster board.

TICKETS PLEASE!
(Welcome and Bible Connection)

- ■ *Objective: To excite children's interest and connect how important encouragement is in daily life with the Bible Truth, children will write encouraging words.*

Welcome Time Activity: Encouragement Bumper Stickers

■ *Materials: 4" x 10" strips of paper, crayons or markers, tape*

As children arrive, invite them to decorate a bulletin board or piece of poster board (or a wall) with bumper stickers. Their bumper stickers should be sayings that encourage, like, "Good Job!" "You Can Do It!" and "Way to Go!" Helpers can assist younger children with writing. When everyone has arrived, call the children to the lesson area.

Sharing Time and Bible Connection

Introduce today's lesson by discussing the following questions. As you talk, give every child the opportunity to say something. Ask for a volunteer and give the child a simple task, like untying a loose knot or organizing some crayons by color. Tell the class their role is to encourage the child up front, and to cheer and clap when the task is finished. Helpers can model this for children to get them participating wholeheartedly.

■ Ask the child who did the task: **Did you feel like the class was on your side and helped you get this job done because they encouraged you?**

■ **How would you have felt if everyone had been completely quiet while you did the job, or ignored you?** Thank the volunteer and continue.

■ **Cheering for someone or showing your appreciation is a type of encouragement. When have you felt encouraged by someone?**

■ **Tell about a time you encouraged someone.**

Signal the helper waiting outside to hurry in urgently and hand you the Mission Files. The helper should say with drama: **You've been given a mission!** Say: **Wow! Another mission! Let's see what we're supposed to do today.** Take out file #6 from the Mission File Book and ask someone to read it aloud. **To complete our mission today, we need to study the lives of two people—Barnabas and Betty Greene. We have to discover whether <u>God loves to encourage His missionaries</u>. What do you think?** Let children respond. **Let's find out!**

ALL ABOARD FOR BIBLE TRUTH   Acts 4:36–37; 9:26–28; 12:25–15:41
(Bible Discover and Learn Time)

■ *Objective: Children will study Acts 4:36–37; 9:26–28; and Acts 12:25—15:41 to better understand the lives of Barnabas and Betty Greene, and discover that God loves to encourage His missionaries.*

■ *Materials: 2 balloons for each child (not blown up), permanent markers*

Before we get started, I need to give you something. Hand out a Barnabas balloon to each child. **How does it feel when someone gives you encouragement? Doesn't it make you feel happy and light inside, almost like you're floating?**

During the story of Barnabas, blow some air into your balloon every time I talk about something encouraging. Demonstrate by blowing a few puffs of air into a balloon. Let the children practice. Whenever you see (+), prompt children to blow into their balloons.

The book of Acts in the Bible tells us about a man named Barnabas. He came from an island called Cyprus. His name means "Son of Encouragement." (+)

At this time, Jesus had already come to earth, been crucified, and had risen again. After Jesus went back to heaven, many people became followers of Jesus and these people were called Christians. They lived together and shared all they had. Barnabas was a part of this group of new Christians. The Bible tells us that Barnabas sold a field and gave all the money to the disciples. This was a big encouragement. (+)

Do you remember Paul? When he was a young man, he was very angry with Christians and had some of them arrested. The Christians were afraid of him! When Paul himself became a Christian, people were still afraid. They didn't believe he was really a follower of Jesus. Barnabas took a big chance, and became Paul's friend. He brought Paul to the disciples and convinced them that Paul really did follow Jesus now. The disciples trusted Barnabas and accepted Paul as one of their group. Was this encouraging to Paul? (+)

Barnabas and Paul traveled together, telling many people about Jesus. For awhile a young man named John Mark worked with them too, but then he left. Paul didn't like that. In Paul and Barnabas' second journey, Barnabas wanted to take John Mark with them, but Paul said no. Because Barnabas believed in John Mark, he decided to travel with him. They worked together to take the news about Jesus to many people. Because Barnabas wanted to encourage John Mark, John Mark became a strong missionary, too. (+) How big are your balloons?

Direct children to let the air out of their Barnabas balloons and set them down. Pass out a "Betty" balloon to every child and have them continue as with their "Barnabas" balloon.

Our second missionary is Betty Greene. Raise your hand if you know what you want to be when you grow up. When Betty was growing up, all she wanted to do was fly airplanes. She was excited about using an airplane to spread the story of Jesus. And she wasn't the only one with this dream! She met several other people who wanted to use airplanes for missionary work. (+) They decided to make a club, the Christian Airman's Missionary Fellowship. Their work would be to use airplanes to fly missionaries to their faraway work and bring them the supplies they needed. (+)

Betty worked hard to help the organization get started and did a lot of the paperwork. There was only one problem; what do you think it was? They didn't have an airplane! Betty and her group prayed and waited. When people heard about what this group wanted to do, they started to send money to help out. (+)

Finally Betty's group bought their first airplane. **Guess who was their first pilot?** Let children answer. **Betty Greene! Betty spent many years flying supplies and missionaries around the world, so the missionaries did not have to wait months to get the things that they needed. (+) A few of the places where Betty traveled to encourage missionaries were Mexico, Peru, Nigeria, and the Sudan. She helped hundreds of missionaries, just by using an airplane and doing what God wanted her to do.** Ask children to set both their balloons on the table.

Both Barnabas and Betty were missionaries who encouraged other missionaries. They're examples of how <u>God loves to encourage his missionaries</u>.

Let's add them to our map. **Barnabas was from Cyprus.** Place the "Barnabas" pushpin in Cyprus. **Barnabas traveled with Paul and John Mark to Jerusalem and Antioch.** Stick pushpins in Jerusalem and in Antioch (middle of Turkey) and draw lines from Cyprus to each location.

Betty Greene grew up in Washington. Place the "Betty" pushpin in Washington. **She traveled all over the world encouraging the missionaries. Some of the places she went were Mexico, Peru, Nigeria and Sudan.** Stick pushpins in those countries. Draw lines from Washington to each location.

Use the Clues!
(Bible Review)
- ***Materials:*** *Mission Passcard rings, copies of Mission Passcard #6*

Have helpers hand out Mission Passcard rings. Then hand out Mission Passcard #6 which children will place on their rings behind card #5. Ask several older children to volunteer to each ask one review question for the class to answer, based on the card rings. Then ask these questions of the class based on today's stories.
- **What does the name Barnabas mean?** (Son of Encouragement)
- **How did he encourage others?** (he sold some land to help take care of other Christians, he got the disciples to accept Paul, he traveled with John Mark)
- **How did Betty Greene encourage other missionaries?** (she flew the supplies they needed to them)
- **How did God use her?** (to encourage and serve other missionaries)

After the game, have helpers collect the card rings.

BIBLE MEMORY WAYPOINT   Zephaniah 3:17

- ***Objective:*** *Children will hide God's Word in their hearts for guidance, protection, and encouragement.*
- ***Materials:*** *several smooth rocks*

The L**ORD** **your God is with you, he is** <u>**mighty**</u> **to save. He will take great delight in you, he will quiet you with his** <u>**love**</u>**, he will rejoice over** <u>**you**</u> **with singing (Zephaniah 3:17).**

As you teach today's Bible memory verse phrase by phrase, demonstrate the ASL motions for the underlined words and have children do the motions with you. You can learn the words for each lesson at these websites:

- **http://commtechlab.msu.edu/sites/aslweb/browser.htm**
- **http://www.lifeprint.com**

If you choose, delegate the teaching of the memory verse to a helper who will learn the ASL signs and teach them weekly. Demonstrate the ASL motions as you teach the verse, and have children do the motions with you.

Let students practice the signs first. Then pass out the rocks in random order as children form a circle. Ask several children to sign the words; those holding a rock will say their word of the verse as the class progresses through the verse. This will be challenging. Have children pass the rocks around the circle, then repeat the process.

PRAYER STATION

- *Objective: Children will explore and practice prayer for themselves in small groups.*
- *Materials: Copies of* StationMaster Card #6 *for each helper*

Break into small groups of three to five children. Assign a teen or adult helper to each small group and give each helper a copy of *StationMaster Card #6* (see Resources, 93) with ideas for group discussion and prayer.

SNACK STOP: SUDANESE SWEETS (Optional)

If you plan to provide a snack, this is an ideal time to serve it.

- *Materials: bananas, raisins, small cups, knife, spoons*

Betty Greene encouraged the missionaries in many places, including the country of Sudan in Africa. Sudanese people like sweets. This dessert is eaten with figs in Sudan, but we're having it with just the bananas and raisins. Chop the bananas, spoon some into each cup and top with some raisins.
Note: Always be aware of children with food allergies and have another option ready.

APPLICATION

■ **Objective:** *Children will have opportunities to show how the lesson works in their own lives through activities and take-home papers.*

Some children's ministries may allow children to play outside at this point. If yours does not, choose one of the following activities.

 Looking Up!

■ **Materials:** *children's 'Barnabas' and 'Betty' balloons from All Aboard for Bible Truth, clock with second hand*

Have the children blow up their two balloons and tie them, with assistance as needed. When you say, "Go," everyone should hit their balloons up in the air. Students should help each other keep the balloons in the air. If you desire, time how long the class can do this. Students can try as many times as they want to beat their best record. After the first round, remind students that sometimes it takes work to be encouraging to others, but it can also be fun and rewarding, like trying to keep balloons in the air.

 African Tie Dye

■ **Materials:** *heavy duty paper towels, string, water, blue food coloring, bowls, old towels or cookie cooling racks*

This ancient craft is an African tradition. Add blue food coloring to bowls half filled with water until the water is a rich blue. Demonstrate how to fan-fold a paper towel back and forth, until the paper is completely folded. Tightly tie pieces of string around the folded paper in several places. Quickly dip the tied towel into the bowl, then lay on the racks or towels until dry. Once dry, cut off the string and unfold to reveal the tie dye design.

 ON THE FAST TRACK! *(Take-home Papers)*

Award trips to the treasure box for children who brought back a signed ticket. Hand out the *On the Fast Track!* papers and encourage children to do the work and learn the verse at home. **When you take your *On the Fast Track!* paper home, you can do the activities and learn the verse. Then ask a parent to sign the ticket. When you bring the ticket back next week, you'll get a prize from the treasure box.**

Before they leave, give children their tie-dyed projects if they made them.

LESSON SEVEN: What Did You Say?

Luke · Cameron Townsend

Memory Verse:

Your <u>word</u> is a lamp to my <u>feet</u> and a <u>light</u> for my path (Psalm 119:105).

Bible Basis:

Luke 1:1–4; Acts 1:1–2; 20:5–12

Bible Truth:

Some missionaries write down God's Word for others to read.

You Will Need:

- ☐ pushpins
- ☐ cardstock or stiff paper
- ☐ 1 poster board
- ☐ Mission Files
- ☐ Mission Passcard #7
- ☐ binder rings with Mission Passcard sets
- ☐ *On the Fast Track! #7* take-homes
- ☐ *StationMaster Card #7*
- ☐ world map
- ☐ cookies
- ☐ *(Optional)* treasure box
- ☐ *(Optional)* Snack: fresh flour tortillas, butter or honey
- ☐ *(Optional)* Activity #1: masking tape
- ☐ *(Optional)* Activity #2: plastic hollow Easter eggs, confetti, crepe paper, tape

When you see this icon, it means preparation will take more than five minutes.

GET SET!
(Lesson Preparation)

- ■ Make a copy of *On the Fast Track! #7* take-home paper for each child.
- ■ Make a copy of *StationMaster Card #7* for each helper.
- ■ Photocopy, fold, and hole punch Mission Passcard #7 on cardstock or stiff paper for each child.
- ■ Cut quarter-sized circles out of cardstock. Write the name "Luke" on one circle and "Cameron Townsend" on the other. Glue each circle to the head of a pushpin.
- ■ Make a copy of the coded message (see Resources, 88) for each child. *(Solution: Solve this then come up front and pick out a cookie!)*
- ■ *(Optional)* Activity #1: make a masking tape line at both ends of the hall or classroom.
- ■ Make confetti or collect hole punched holes for Activity #2, if using.
- ■ Arrange with a StationMaster helper to bring in the Mission Files with urgency and drama during the Sharing Time today and following weeks.
- ■ Print this week's memory verse on the poster board.

TICKETS PLEASE!
(Welcome and Bible Connection)

- ■ **Objective:** *To excite children's interest and connect the concept of translating an unknown language with the Bible Truth, children will decode a message.*

Welcome Time Activity: Decode a Message

■ *Materials:* *copies of coded message for each child, pencils, cookies*

As children arrive, hand them a copy of the code and pencils. Direct them to the numbers printed on the chalkboard. Helpers can encourage them to figure out the secret message. Let helpers suggest that the numbers don't make any sense. Then children can translate what the numbers stand for. When everyone has arrived, call the children to the lesson area.

Sharing Time and Bible Connection

Introduce today's lesson with an object lesson and discussion. As you talk, give every child the opportunity to say something.

Ask two children to come forward. Greet them in a foreign language if you know one, or make up a sentence in a meaningless but convincing "language." Ask the children if they understood what you said. Then ask the rest of the class if they understood.

■ **Why couldn't** (names of two children) **understand what I said?**
■ **Have you ever been to a country where a different language is spoken?**
■ **How would you feel if everyone around you spoke with words you didn't understand?**
■ **Some people feel the same way when it comes to God's Word. They speak one language, and the Bible is written in a different language.**

Signal the helper waiting outside to hurry in urgently and hand you the Mission Files. The helper should say with drama: **You've been given a mission!**

Cool! We've got another mission! Let's see what our assignment is for today. Recruit a volunteer to take the Mission #7 folder from the Mission Files and read it to the class. **To complete our mission today, we need to investigate the lives of two people—Luke and Cameron Townsend. We need to find out why <u>some missionaries write down God's Word for others to read</u>.**

ALL ABOARD FOR BIBLE TRUTH   Luke 1:1-4; Acts 1:1-2; 20:5-12
(Bible Discover and Learn Time)

■ *Objective:* *Children will study Luke 1:1–4; Acts 1:1–2; and Acts 20:5–12 to see how missionaries like Luke and Cameron Townsend have written down God's Word so others can understand it.*
■ *Materials:* *Butcher Paper, markers or crayons, photocopies of coded cookie message, pencils, cookies, code written on the chalkboard from the Welcome Time activity*

A man named Luke lived during Bible times. He was a doctor and a writer. In fact, he wrote down the story of Jesus' life in the Bible which we call the book of Luke, and he wrote the book of Acts too. The Bible tells us why he wrote. Many people who were with Jesus wrote stories about the things they saw Jesus do and say. Luke checked out all the stories. He wrote down the true stories so his friend, Theophilus, would know about Jesus.

Luke also traveled around with Paul on some of his missionary trips. He saw first hand what happened in the days after Jesus' death and resurrection. Luke wrote those things down too. **Why do you think it was important for Luke to write down the things he saw and heard?** Help children come to the conclusion that when you write down a story, it is there to read and remember forever. If someone forgets what happened, you can go to the writing to get the truth.

To find out why it's important to write down truth from first hand experience, we're going to do an activity.

Divide the class into three groups. Tell the following story from Acts 20:5–12 to one group while helpers keep the other two groups occupied elsewhere in or outside of the room with a game or song. After you tell the story to this first group, bring in group 2 and have group 1 retell the story as they know it. Then, send group 1 out and bring in group 3. Have group 2 tell the story to group 3. Finally, gather the whole class together again and ask group 3 to tell what they heard. Ask the other groups what they think they heard. Then tell the story again the original way.

The story of Acts 20:5–12

In the book of Acts Luke wrote about Paul's visit to the city of Troas. "On the first day of the week we came together to share food together. Paul spoke to the people. He kept on talking until midnight. There were many lamps in the upstairs room where we were meeting. A young man named Eutychus was sitting near a window. He fell asleep while Paul talked on and on. He was so deeply asleep that he fell out the window and down to the ground. He was dead! Paul went down, threw himself on the young man and put his arms around him. "Don't be alarmed," he said. "He's alive!" Then he went upstairs again and ate. The people took the young man home alive and were amazed."

Summarize the results of the activity. **You all did a great job. Did you hear how when a story is passed from person to person, or from group to group, it can change. People hear some things and forget some of the details or may remember them differently. This is what the actual story was.** Repeat the story as originally told.

Luke did a great job of writing down the story of Jesus and his experiences with Paul. He wrote them so we will know the truth of what happened and can learn about who God is.

Cameron Townsend was another writer and lived about 100 years ago. Cameron wanted to become a missionary so he went to the country of Guatemala. **What language do we speak in our country?** Let children answer. In Guatemala they spoke many languages. Cameron was surprised at that! But he was even more surprised to learn that there was no Bible for the people to read in all those languages.

Cameron wanted everybody to be able to read the Bible in their own language and understand what God had done for them. It would be a lot of work. Remember how much work it was to make the code into words and earn a cookie? Imagine how hard it would be to make the words of the Bible into a different language. He would need help! Cameron gathered a group of people to put the Bible in different languages. His group was called Wycliffe Bible Translators.

Today, Wycliffe Bible Translators has written the New Testament into more than 500 different languages. Guess how many more they're working on? 1,000 more languages! Cameron Townsend did what God asked and wrote God's word so others can read it.

Luke was born in Antioch. Place the "Luke" pushpin in Syria. **Our story today took place in Troas.** Stick a tack in Troas (northwest Turkey). Draw a line between the tacks.

Cameron Townsend lived in California. Place the "Cameron" pushpin in Los Angeles. **His first missionary trip was to Guatemala.** Stick a tack in Guatemala. Draw a line between the two locations.

Use the Clues!
(Bible Review)
- ▪ **Materials:** *Mission Passcard rings, copies of Mission Passcard #7*

Have helpers hand out Mission Passcard rings. Then hand out Mission Passcard #7. For fun, divide the class into a boys' and a girls' team. Alternate teams as you ask review questions. Start with questions from today's lesson and then review previous lessons. Allow children to use their cards to answer.

- ▪ **What did Luke do?** (Luke wrote about Jesus' life so people would know the truth)
- ▪ **How did God use him?** (God used Luke to tell many people about Jesus' life and what happened after His resurrection)
- ▪ **What did Cameron do?** (Cameron translated God's Word into languages that didn't have the Bible yet.)
- ▪ **Why did Cameron translate the New Testament?** (he wanted to make sure that everyone could read God's Word)
Have helpers collect the card rings.

BIBLE MEMORY WAYPOINT   Psalms 119:105

- ▪ *Objective: Children will hide God's Word in their hearts for guidance, protection, and encouragement.*

Your <u>word</u> is a lamp to my <u>feet</u> and a <u>light</u> for my path (Psalm 119:105).

As you teach today's Bible memory verse phrase by phrase, demonstrate the ASL motions for thr under,ined words and have children do the motions with you. You can learn the signs for these words at these websites:

- ▪ http://commtechlab.msu.edu/sites/aslweb/browser.htm
- ▪ http://www.lifeprint.com

If you choose, delegate the teaching of the memory verse to a helper who will learn the ASL signs and teach them weekly.

Practice the verse phrase by phrase until it is familiar. Then let children "perform" the verse by groups: boys, girls, kids wearing pants, etc.

PRAYER STATION

- **Objective:** *Children will explore and practice prayer for themselves in small groups.*
- **Materials:** *Copies of* StationMaster Card #7 *for each helper*

Break into small groups. Assign a teen or adult helper to each small group and give each helper a copy of *StationMaster Card #7* (see Resources, 93) with ideas for group discussion and prayer.

SNACK STOP: TORTILLA TIME (Optional)

If you plan to provide a snack, this is an ideal time to serve it.

- **Materials:** *fresh flour tortillas, butter or honey*

Warm the tortillas if possible (wrap in a damp towel and microwave or heat in an oven) and serve with butter or honey. **In Guatemala, where Cameron Townsend first wrote the Bible in different languages, they like to eat flatbreads like these tortillas. Guatemalans also eat lots of beans, tropical fruits like bananas and grapefruit, and meat like chicken.**

APPLICATION

- **Objective:** *Children will have opportunities to show how the lesson works in their own lives through activities and take-home papers.*

Some children's ministries may allow children to play outside at this point. If yours does not, choose one of the following activities.

Note: Always be aware of children with food allergies and provide another option.

Say What? Relay

Divide the class into two teams. Give each the name of a foreign place or people, e.g. the Tikis, the Javas, or the Maoris. Divide each team into two parts. The two parts will line up behind the masking tape start lines at opposite ends of the room, facing each other. To start, whisper a sentence (for example: When palm trees drop their coconuts, do they bounce?) into the ear of the first players on one side of the room. When you say go, these two run to their teammates at the other end of the room and whisper the sentence to the first person in line. Then those teammates run to the opposite line and repeat the process. Continue until everybody has had a turn. Players who have had their turn will go to the end of the line and sit down. After both teams finished, have the last player who heard the sentence repeat it aloud. The team who was the quickest and kept the message closest to its original form wins.

Confetti Eggs

■ *Materials: plastic hollow Easter eggs, confetti or cut-up bits of colorful tissue paper or hole punched bits, crepe paper, tape*

Let each child add confetti to one half of an egg, then place the other half on top. Helpers can assist with wrapping a short strip of crepe paper around the center where the halves meet, and taping it in place. Tell the children how in Guatemala, there's a holiday near Easter when children take empty egg shells, fill them with confetti, and close them with crepe paper. Then they play a joke on someone by smashing the egg on their head, getting confetti all over the person's hair. (Discourage carrying out this aspect of the tradition!)

ON THE FAST TRACK! *(Take-home Papers)*

Award trips to the treasure box for children who brought back a signed ticket. Hand out the *On the Fast Track!* papers and encourage children to do the work and learn the verse at home. **When you take your *On the Fast Track!* paper home, you can do the activities and learn the verse. Then ask a parent to sign the ticket. When you bring the ticket back next week, you'll get a prize from the treasure box.**

Before they leave, give children their confetti egg if they made one.

LESSON EIGHT: Short Term Missionaries

Philip · Short term missionary

Memory Verse:

Be <u>kind</u> and compassionate to one another, forgiving each other, just as in <u>Christ</u> God forgave <u>you</u> (Ephesians 4:32).

Bible Basis:

Acts 8:26–40

Bible Truth:

Missionaries sometimes go on short journeys.

You Will Need:

- ☐ pushpins
- ☐ cardstock or stiff paper
- ☐ 1 poster board
- ☐ Mission Files
- ☐ Mission Passcard #8
- ☐ rings with Mission Passcard sets
- ☐ world map
- ☐ a connection with a local short-term missionary, preferably from your own congregation
- ☐ fresh leaves
- ☐ colored pencils
- ☐ *On the Fast Track! #8* take-home paper
- ☐ *StationMaster Card #8*
- ☐ *(Optional)* treasure box
- ☐ *(Optional)* Snack: fresh sourdough bread, rolling pins or clean cans, paper towels, cottage cheese (optional)
- ☐ *(Optional)* Activity #1: blindfolds, objects to make a maze
- ☐ *(Optional)* Activity #2: 8" squares of silver foil wrapping paper, black construction paper, scissors, pencils, glue; cardstock; African cross pattern (see Resources, 89)

When you see this icon, preparation will take more than five minutes.

GET SET!
(Lesson Preparation)

- ■ Make a copy of *On the Fast Track! #8* take-home paper for each child.
- ■ Make a copy of *StationMaster Card #8* for each helper.
- ■ Photocopy, fold, and hole punch Mission Passcard #8 on cardstock or stiff paper for each child. Write the name of your short-term missionary on it.
- ■ Cut quarter-sized circles out of cardstock. Write the name "Philip" on one circle and *(name of your short-term missionary)* on the other. Glue each circle to the head of a pushpin.
- ■ Make contact with local short-term missionary who can come to your class to briefly share the highlights of his/her missionary work, or acquire their story to tell yourself.
- ■ Collect a variety of fresh leaves with textures that will make good rubbings, if using the Welcome Time Activity.
- ■ *(Optional)* Activity #1: Make a sample game board out of one manila folder and 2" x 3" cards according to the directions for Activity #1.
- ■ *(Optional)* Activity #2: Enlarge African cross pattern to measure 8" high. Make several cross patterns out of cardstock.
- ■ Arrange with a StationMaster helper to bring in the Mission Files with urgency and drama during the Sharing Time today.
- ■ Print this week's memory verse on the poster board.

TICKETS PLEASE!
(Welcome and Bible Connection)

■ *Objective: To excite children's interest and connect the differences and similarities among missionary trips with the Bible Truth, children will make two kinds of art using leaves.*

Welcome Time Activity: Rubbings and Drawings

■ *Materials: paper, colored pencils, flat tree leaves*
As children arrive, invite them to where you have paper, pencils and leaves set out. Ask each child to make two different pictures of leaves. For one, do rubbings of leaves by laying the paper over the bumpier side of a leaf and coloring with the side of a pencil. The leaf impression should show up on the paper. Then the child should draw freehand some leaves that look like the one they rubbed. When everyone has arrived, call the children to the lesson area.

Sharing Time and Bible Connection

Introduce today's lesson by discussing the following questions. As you talk, give every child the opportunity to say something. Hold up pictures made during the Welcome Time Activity.

■ **Look at these two types of art with leaves. How are they the same?** (they all were made with the leaves, they leaves are made with pencil)
■ **How are the drawings different?** (the rubbings look more alike, the freehand leaves are all different, the rubbings were faster to make)
■ **What are some things that take a long time to make or do?**
■ **What kinds of things take a short time to make or do?**

Missionary work is the same in some ways. All missionaries go to where God sends them so more people can learn about Jesus and eternal life in heaven. But missionaries do their work in different ways. Some missionaries go out for many years, and some go for a short time.

Help students connect their discussion to the Bible story from Acts 8:26-40. Signal the helper waiting outside to hurry in urgently and hand you the Mission Files. The helper should say with drama: **You've been given a mission!** Say: **Wow! Another mission! Let's see what our assignment is for today.** Ask a child to take out Mission #8 file from the Mission File Book and read it aloud. **To complete our mission today, we need to study the lives of two people—Philip and** (*name of your short-term missionary*). **We need to find out if <u>mission trips are long or short</u>.**

ALL ABOARD FOR BIBLE TRUTH   Acts 8:26–40
(Bible Discover and Learn Time)

- ■ **Objective:** *Children will study Acts 8:26–40 to learn about the missionary work of Philip and (short-term missionary), realizing that some missionaries go on short journeys.*
- ■ **Materials:** *"Philip" and short term missionary pushpins, world map, extra pushpins*

Sometimes being a missionary doesn't mean you go to a foreign country to live there your whole life. Sometimes God sends Christians on short trips to foreign countries. That's the way God used Philip.

Ask for volunteers and assign roles for an angel, Philip, the Ethiopian man, and a chariot driver. Have the volunteers stand up front with you. You'll read the Bible passage (from a kid-friendly translation) and pause at spots while the actors perform the story in actions and words. When done, thank the actors and have them sit down again.

Philip lived hundreds of years ago and in a country far away. But *(short term missionary)* **is from our own area. How many of you know** *(missionary)***? His/her story is a lot like Philip's. God told him/her what to do when He needed him or her to do it, and** *(missionary)* **obeyed God.**

If the missionary can visit your class to share his/her work in 3 to 5 minutes, have the person do so now. You might consider doing a short question-and-answer interview to conserve time, asking what job God gave them, where they went, what they did, how they saw God work among the people, and how long they were doing that work. If the missionary isn't present in the class, share the essentials of the person's work. Show the person's picture if possible.

Both of these missionaries were sent by God on short journeys. What was the best part of Philip's story? Let the children respond. **How about** *(missionary's)* **story?** Let the children respond. **There are a lot of good parts, but the very best was that because Philip and** *(missionary)* **obeyed God, and many people found out about Jesus. What happens when people hear about Jesus?** Let children respond. **They can choose to be forgiven for their sins and to become His followers.**

Philip was born in Bethsaida. Place the "Philip" pushpin in Galilee, east and north of where the Jordan River meets the Sea of Galilee. **God sent Philip to a desert road between Jerusalem and Gaza to meet the Ethiopian.** Stick pushpin between Jerusalem and Gaza. **Then he went to Azotus.** Stick a pushpin in Ashdod on the coast, across from Jerusalem. **He ended up in Caesarea.** Stick a pushpin on the coast of the Sea of Galilee. Draw lines to show each mission trip.

(Missionary) **lives in** *(location)*. Place a pushpin with the missionary's name on that location. **S/he went as a missionary to** *(location)*. Stick a pushpin on the location. Draw lines to show the mission trip.

Use the Clues!
(Bible Review)

■ **Materials:** *Mission Passcard rings, copies of Mission Passcard #8*

Have helpers hand out Mission Passcard rings. Then hand out Mission Passcard #8 which children will place on their rings behind card #7. Play "Popcorn" to spice up the review. Children sit on the floor as you ask a question. The first one to pop up gets a try at answering. If they can't answer correctly let another child pop up to help them.

■ **Where did Philip hear that someone needed help in finding God?** (God told Philip where to go and who to see)
■ **How did Philip show the Ethiopian man about Jesus?** (he told the man what the Scriptures meant so the Ethiopian man could understand salvation)
■ **How did** *(missionary)* **share God with others?**
■ **What ways Did God use** *(missionary's)* **work in** *(location)*?

After the game, have helpers collect the card rings.

BIBLE MEMORY WAYPOINT   Ephesians 4:32

■ **Objective:** *Children will hide God's Word in their hearts for guidance, protection, and encouragement.*

Be <u>kind</u> and compassionate to one another, forgiving each other, just as in <u>Christ</u> God forgave <u>you</u> (Ephesians 4:32).

As you teach today's Bible memory verse phrase by phrase, demonstrate the ASL motions for the underlined words and have children do the motions with you. You can learn the signs for these words at these websites:

■ http://commtechlab.msu.edu/sites/aslweb/browser.htm
■ http://www.lifeprint.com

If you choose, delegate the teaching of the memory verse to a helper who will learn the ASL signs and teach them weekly.

Have students find partners and face each other. You or the helper teaching the signs will stand at one end of the room so that one partner of each group can see you. As you say the words, both partners will repeat after you. The partner who can see you will repeat the sign after seeing it, so the other partner can learn it. Do this a couple of times. Explain that this is one way missionaries work. They train people so those people can train others to follow Jesus. Affirm the children for being useful to God by teaching Scripture to one another.

PRAYER STATION

- ■ *Objective:* *Children will explore and practice prayer for themselves in small groups.*
- ■ *Materials:* *Copies of* StationMaster Card #8 *for each helper*

Break into small groups of three to five children. Assign a teen or adult helper to each small group and give each helper a copy of *StationMaster Card #8* (see Resources, 94) with ideas for group discussion and prayer.

SNACK STOP: ETHIOPIAN INJERA (Optional)

If you plan to provide a snack, this is an ideal time to serve it.

- ■ *Materials:* *fresh sourdough bread, rolling pins or clean cans, paper towels, cottage cheese (optional)*

Ethiopian food is very different from ours. People in Ethiopia don't use any forks, knives or spoons! They scoop all their food up with a pancake like bread called injera. We can't make that because they have different ingredients in their country. But it tastes kind of like sourdough bread. Give each child a slice or two of bread and let them make a pancake from it by laying the slices on a paper towel and rolling them with a rolling pin or can. They can scoop up cottage cheese in the Ethiopian manner if you choose and they want to try it. To eat the "injera" the Ethiopian way, they should tear off bites one by one.

Note: Always be aware of children with food allergies and have another option on hand if necessary.

APPLICATION

- ■ *Objective:* *Children will have opportunities to show how the lesson works in their own lives through activities and take-home papers.*

Some children's ministries may allow children to play outside at this point. If yours does not, choose one of the following activities.

What Is My Move?

■ *Materials: blindfolds, objects to make a maze (pillows, chairs, wooden plank, etc.)*

Sometimes God tells us every step that we need to take. We're going to play a game to practice listening to directions. Make a maze on the floor of an open area. You might have children walk around a table, go under a chair, stand on a plank, and go over a pillow. Pair up an older child with a younger one. Blindfold the older one and stand him at a "start line." The other child will stand on the sideline and call out instructions to guide his partner through the maze. When the partner has successfully completed the maze, partners may switch jobs. Add to the fun, by having 3 children go through the maze at the same time while their partners all call out instructions at the same time!

Ethiopian Crosses

■ *Materials: 8-inch squares of silver foil wrapping paper, black construction paper, scissors, glue, symmetrical cross patterns (see Resources, 89).*

The children will create a **maskal**, a fancy silver cross that people in Ethiopia wear as necklaces or carry in church. Give each child a square of foil wrapping paper. Set cross patterns in the center where everyone can reach them. Have children trace a cross onto their squares of foil. Cut out the cross. Then, make an exact horizontal fold. Fold again to make an exact vertical fold. Cut small geometric shapes from the folded edges, the same way you would to make paper snowflakes. Unfold the cross carefully and glue it on a sheet of black construction paper.

ON THE FAST TRACK! *(Take-home Papers)*

(Optional) treasure box. Award trips to the treasure box for children who brought back a signed ticket. Hand out the *On the Fast Track!* papers and encourage children to do the work and learn the verse at home. **When you take your *On the Fast Track!* paper home, you can do the activities and learn the verse. Then ask a parent to sign the ticket. When you bring the ticket back next week, you'll get a prize from the treasure box.**

Before they leave, give children their take-home papers and Ethiopian crosses if they made one.

LESSON NINE: Performing Miracles!

Memory Verse:
Jesus looked at them and said, "With <u>man</u> this is <u>impossible</u>, but with <u>God</u> all things are <u>possible</u>" (Matthew 19:26).

Bible Basis:
Acts 12:4–17

Bible Truth:
God can do miracles anytime and anyplace.

Peter • Jonathan Goforth

You Will Need:

- ☐ pushpins
- ☐ cardstock or stiff paper
- ☐ 1 poster board
- ☐ Mission Files
- ☐ world map
- ☐ two paper chains
- ☐ Mission Passcard #9
- ☐ binder rings with Mission Passcard sets
- ☐ *On the Fast Track!* #9 take-home paper
- ☐ *StationMaster Card* #9
- ☐ (Optional) treasure box
- ☐ (Optional) Snack: Chinese almond cookies and/or sliced oranges
- ☐ (Optional) Activity #1: blindfolds for half the class
- ☐ (Optional) Activity #2: photocopied tangram pattern, scissors, envelopes

 When you see this icon, it means preparation will take more than five minutes.

GET SET!
(Lesson Preparation)

- ■ Make a copy of *On the Fast Track!* #9 take-home paper for each child.
- ■ Make a copy of *StationMaster Card* #9 for each helper.
- ■ Photocopy, fold, and hole punch Mission Passcard #9 on cardstock or stiff paper for each child.
- ■ Cut quarter-sized circles out of cardstock. Write the name "Peter" on one circle and "Jonathan Goforth" on the other. Glue each circle to the head of a pushpin.
- ■ Make two paper chains, each about 2 feet long.
- ■ If using the Welcome Time Activity, divide a length of butcher paper into two sections. Label one "Miracles" and the other "Magic."
- ■ Photocopy the tangram pattern (see Resources, 89) and cut one out as a sample, if using Activity #2.
- ■ Arrange with a StationMaster helper to bring in the Mission Files with urgency and drama during the Sharing Time today and following weeks.
- ■ Print this week's memory verse on the poster board.

TICKETS PLEASE!
(Welcome and Bible Connection)

- ■ **Objective:** *To excite children's interest and connect their understanding about miracles with the Bible Truth, they will compare miracles to magic.*

Welcome Time Activity: Miracles or Magic?

■ *Materials: Miracles or Magic butcher paper, markers or pencils*
    As children arrive, direct them to a length of butcher paper on the table or floor. Helpers at the area will greet children and invite them to write or draw an example of a miracle and an example of magic. Have helpers engage the children in chatting about what they're drawing. Be sure that children clearly understand that magic is not real; it is done with tricks for the entertainment of an audience. When everyone has arrived, call the children to the lesson area.

Sharing Time and Bible Connection

Introduce today's lesson by using the Welcome Time Activity as a discussion starter. Ask a few children to show what they wrote or drew and how they knew which was a miracle and what was magic.

■ **Who else has something to share about miracles?**
■ **When do we see miracles happen?** (when God wants to show His power or care, when God is working in someone's life or in nature)
■ **How do you think God might use miracles in places where missionaries are working?**

   Miracles are actions God does to show His power or care. They're things that are impossible for people. We can't explain how they happen. Magic is often done with tricks and doesn't show us anything about God or His amazing ability and wisdom.
    After discussion time, help your students connect their discussion to the Bible story they are about to hear from Acts 12:4–17. Signal the helper waiting outside to hurry in urgently and hand you the Mission Files. The helper should say with drama: **You've been given a mission!** Say: **Let's see what our assignment is for today.** Choose a child to take out the Mission #9 folder from the Mission File Book and read it aloud. **To complete our mission today, we learn about the lives of two people—Peter and Jonathan Goforth. We need to find out why <u>God might do miracles as His missionaries work for Him</u>.**

📖 ALL ABOARD FOR BIBLE TRUTH   Acts 12:4-17
(Bible Discover and Learn Time)

■ *Objective: Children will study Peter in Acts 12:4–17 and hear about a modern missionary to realize that God can do miracles anytime and anyplace as His missionaries work for Him.*
■ *Materials: two paper chains, "Peter" and Jonathan" pushpins, extra pushpins, world map*

Create a prison by using chairs or tables set close together to give the idea of a jail cell. Ask one helper to be Peter inside the cell. Use a paper chain to "bind" the helper's hands and feet. Ask two children to be guards who stand on either side of Peter. Then ask 16 kids, or the rest of your class, to take up positions standing guard around the prison.

Have any of the missionaries we've learned about been in jail? (Yes, Paul and Silas.) Missionaries sometimes get in trouble for telling people that Jesus can forgive them their sins! Today's missionary is Peter, and he was in jail, too. What did Peter do wrong to end up being a prisoner? The Bible says he didn't do anything wrong. He was a part of the first church of Christians who were sharing about God with people. And the king, who was named Herod, didn't like that. So he put Peter in jail. Peter is chained with two chains, and has two guards next to him, and then there were 16 other guards around the outside of the prison cell. Things looked really bad for Peter.

At this time, the Jewish people were celebrating a holiday called Passover. King Herod wanted to wait until after their holiday to put Peter on trial. Herod wanted to find a reason to kill Peter for preaching about Jesus. On the night before the trial, Peter was sleeping between two soldiers. He had two sets of chains on him, and there were guards at the door. Do you think Peter can escape? Let children respond. **Will Peter go on trial, or stay in prison, or will he die?** Take a vote with children choosing what they think will happen.

Let's wait to hear what will happen with Peter, while I tell you about Jonathan Goforth. He grew up in Canada, got married and had a family. And he felt God sending him to China as a missionary. At that time, Chinese people mostly didn't like having foreigners with their unusual ideas. Then Chinese rulers decided all the foreigners—people who weren't from China—had to leave.

Just getting out of China was really difficult. There were no cars, so first Jonathan's family rode in a wagon pulled by oxen. They bumped over roads a long way to the ocean. They were planning to take a boat to get back to Canada. The Chinese people were mad at the foreigners. Mobs of people from the towns around would come out and throw rocks and sticks at them. Raise your hand if you've been hit with a rock. Jonathan was hit in the head by a rock and hurt badly.

One night an ox-cart driver overheard soldiers in a village talking. The soldiers acted like they were going to protect and help the missionaries, but they really were going to lead them down a road where an ambush was planned. Who knows what an ambush is? Let the children respond. **An ambush is a surprise attack. The soldiers planned to kill the missionaries.**

Early the next morning, while it was still dark, the soldiers came for the missionaries. The missionaries had no choice—they had to follow the soldiers even though they knew the plan. Suddenly they realized that a friend and Jonathan's oldest son were missing from their group. They stopped the caravan and started to search. They searched for hours.

It started to get light out. They had nowhere else to search, so the group had to go on without those two. Jonathan didn't want to leave his son behind. What do you think is going to happen to Jonathan Goforth and his family?

Both Peter and Jonathan found themselves in bad situations. But they were serving the all-powerful God! God chose to do a miracle for Peter. Send another helper into the "cell" to bring out Peter. **First, an angel woke him up in prison, told Peter to get up, and follow him. The chains just fell off him, and he followed the angel out of the cell, past the guards, and through the gate of the city. At first, Peter thought that he was in a dream, but when the angel left him, he realized that it wasn't. God has done a miracle for this missionary.**

And now let's find out what happened to Jonathan Goforth. While the group searched for Jonathan's son, the soldiers crawled into the back of a cart and fell asleep. The missionaries let them sleep as they left the village. When the missionaries came to a place where the road went in two different directions, the missionaries didn't know which road to take. So they let the oxen decide! Several hours later, the soldiers woke up. They started yelling and hitting each other. The missionaries had taken the road away from the ambush. God used some animals to keep his missionaries safe! Once they reached the next town, the friend and Jonathan's son caught up with them. God had kept them safe, too.

God miraculously saved Peter and Jonathan from death. <u>God can do miracles anytime and anyplace</u> **as His missionaries work for Him.**

Where did Peter serve God? In Galilee. Place the "Peter" pushpin in Galilee. **Jonathan Goforth grew up in Ontario, Canada.** Place the "Jonathan" pushpin in Ontario, Canada. **He and his family were missionaries in China.** Stick a pushpin around Shanghai, China. Draw a line between the tacks.

Use the Clues!
(Bible Review)
- *Materials: Mission Passcards rings, Mission Passcard #9*

Helpers hand out Mission Passcard rings. Then have helpers hand out Mission Passcard #9. Briefly check for understanding of today's lesson with these questions:

- **Why was Peter in jail?** (because King Herod didn't like him telling people about Jesus)
- **What miracle did God do for Peter?** (He freed him from jail)
- **What miracle did God perform for Jonathan Goforth and his family?** (He protected them from the angry Chinese people, saved them from an ambush that might have gotten them killed)
- **What's the difference between God's miracles and people's magic?** (Miracles aren't tricks, they're actions only God can make happen because of His power)

Then, review other lessons by playing the "Show Me" game. As you quiz the class about the lives of people from previous lessons, ask children to flip to the card that tells about that person, and then hold up that card and show you. For example, **Show me the person God freed from prison with a miracle.** Children will flip over to the "Peter" card and hold it up to show you. Play several rounds of this game and then have helpers collect card sets for use next week.

BIBLE MEMORY WAYPOINT   Matthew 19:26

■ *Objective: Children will hide God's Word in their hearts for guidance, protection, and encouragement.*

Jesus looked at them and said, "With <u>man</u> this is <u>impossible</u>, but with <u>God</u> all things are <u>possible</u>" (Matthew 19:26).

As you teach today's Bible memory verse phrase by phrase, demonstrate the ASL motions and have children do the motions with you. You can learn the signs for these words at these websites:

- ■ http://commtechlab.msu.edu/sites/aslweb/browser.htm
- ■ http://www.lifeprint.com

To practice, write the verse on the board, then read it and teach the signs. Erase one key word and repeat the verse with words and signs. Erase two more words and again say and sign the verse. Continue until all the words have been erased.

If you choose, delegate the teaching of the memory verse to a helper who will learn the ASL signs and teach them weekly.

PRAYER STATION

- ■ *Objective: Children will explore and practice prayer for themselves in small groups.*
- ■ *Materials: Copies of* StationMaster Card #9 *for each helper*

Break into small groups of three to five children. Assign a teen or adult helper to each small group and give each helper a copy of *StationMaster Card #9* (see Resources, 94) with ideas for group discussion and prayer.

SNACK STOP: CHINESE SWEET TREATS (Optional)

If you plan to provide a snack, this is an ideal time to serve it.

■ *Materials: Chinese almond cookies (purchased) or sliced oranges*

Ask children if they've had Chinese food before. Let them describe what they've eaten. Explain that the Chinese people don't eat the same kinds of sweets or desserts that we do. But they do like almond cookies or sliced oranges. Serve what you've chosen and ask the children what foods and treats they are thankful for.

APPLICATION

■ **Objective:** *Children will have opportunities to show how the lesson works in their own lives through activities and take-home papers.*

Some children's ministries may allow children to play outside at this point. If yours does not, choose one of the following activities.

 ## Sneaky Prison Escape

■ **Materials:** *blindfolds for half the class*

Divide the class into two groups. One group will be prison guards who are sleeping; the others will be the prisoners who escape. Blindfold the prison guard group and scatter them throughout the play area. They'll lie down, and pretend to sleep. Prisoners will gather on one side of the room, with the goal of tiptoeing around and through the field of guards. If a guard reaches out and touches a sneaking prisoner, that prisoner is caught and has to sit and wait out the rest of the game. The prisoners' goal is to reach freedom at the opposite side of the room. After the game ends, change roles and play again.

 ## Chinese Tangrams

■ **Materials:** *photocopied tangrams (see Resources, 89), scissors, envelopes*

Hand out a sheet of the copied tangram pattern to each child. Explain that tangrams are Chinese paper puzzles. Each of the 7 shapes is called a tan. Together they make a square. Chinese people enjoy making pictures of everyday objects with their tangrams. Children will cut carefully along the lines to create the 7 geometric shapes. Encourage them to make objects using all 7 pieces and ask a friend to guess what they've made.

You can see some examples online by doing a web search on "tangrams + puzzles."

Give children envelopes to stash their tangrams to take home.

 ## ON THE FAST TRACK! *(Take-home Papers)*

Award trips to the treasure box for children who brought back a signed ticket. Give each child an *On the Fast Track!* paper. **Each week you can take home an *On the Fast Track!* paper and do the activities and practice the memory verse. When you've done those things, ask a parent to sign the ticket** (point it out). **Bring back the ticket and you can take a trip into the treasure box** (hold up box).

Now, who wants take home *On the Fast Track?* Get children excited about doing the weekly activities.

Hand out the children's tangram envelopes if they made them.

LESSON TEN: The Greatest Sacrifice

Memory Verse:

Be <u>strong</u> and courageous. Do not be <u>terrified</u>; do not be discouraged, for the LORD your God will be with <u>you</u> wherever you go (Joshua 1:9).

Bible Truth:

Some missionaries give their lives so others can hear about God.

Bible Basis:

Matthew 4:18–22; Mark 3:13–19; Mark 16:19–20; John 18:1–11; John 21:1–14; Acts 2:1–13; Acts 2:42–47; Acts 8:1–3; Acts 12:1–2

You Will Need:

- ☐ pushpins
- ☐ cardstock or stiff paper
- ☐ 1 poster board
- ☐ Mission Files
- ☐ Mission Passcard #10
- ☐ rings with Mission Passcard sets
- ☐ world map
- ☐ play dough (see recipe on page 30)
- ☐ *On the Fast Track! #10* take-home paper
- ☐ *StationMaster Card #10*
- ☐ (Optional) treasure box
- ☐ (Optional) Snack: toothpicks, fruits cut into bite-size pieces, such as, bananas, watermelon, pineapple, papaya
- ☐ (Optional) Activity #1: copies of parrot art, enlarged to fill the 8½" x 11" page (see Resources, 90); pre-cut colored paper bits, glue sticks
- ☐ (Optional) Activity #2: missionary kits

When you see this icon, it means preparation will take more than five minutes.

GET SET!
(Lesson Preparation)

- ■ Make a copy of *On the Fast Track! #10* take-home paper for each child.
- ■ Make a copy of *StationMaster Card #10* for each helper.
- ■ Photocopy, fold, and hole punch Mission Passcard #10 on cardstock or stiff paper for each child.
- ■ Cut quarter-sized circles out of cardstock. Write the name "James" on one circle and "Jim Elliot" on the other. Glue each circle to the head of a pushpin.
- ■ Photocopy the numbered stories of James and Jim Elliot (see *All Aboard* section) and cut apart into 7 strips.
- ■ Create two Missionary Kits if using Activity #1: Place two sets of identical items in two duffle bags or suitcases. Items can be anything a jungle missionary might wear or use: safari jacket; wide-brimmed hat; cargo pants; pair of boots; Bible with an attached note "Look up today's memory verse, Joshua 1:9;" a spray bottle of water labeled insect repellent that must be sprayed over player's head; "Missionary" I.D. tag in a plastic holder on a neck chain; briefcase with lots of papers in it, etc.
- ■ Photocopy the parrot picture if using Activity #1. ßAlso cut (freehand or with a paper cutter) 1/2" strips of bright paper (purple, red, yellow, blue, orange, etc.). Then cut the strips into half-inch squares to serve as mosaic pieces.
- ■ Arrange with a StationMaster helper to bring in the Mission Files with urgency and drama during the Sharing Time today.
- ■ Print this week's memory verse on the poster board.

TICKETS PLEASE!
(Welcome and Bible Connection)

■ **Objective:** *To excite children's interest and connect what it means to give it all to God with the Bible Truth, children will make play dough figures of things that are important to them.*

Welcome Time Activity: What's Important?

■ **Materials:** *play dough*

As children arrive, invite them to take a chunk of play dough. Ask them to create a model of something that's very important to them. Helpers can engage children in conversation about what they're making. When everyone has arrived, call the children to the lesson area. They should leave their models behind to collect at the end of class.

Sharing Time and Bible Connection

Introduce today's lesson by discussing the following questions. As you talk, give every child the opportunity to say something.

■ **What did you make a model of? What other things are important to you?**
■ **What other things are important to you?** Let children call out ideas.
■ **How would you feel if your most important thing was taken away?**
■ **Would you ever choose to give away this important thing?**

Signal the helper waiting outside to hurry in and hand you the Mission Files. The helper should say: **You've been given a mission!** Say: **Wow! Let's see what we're supposed to do today.** Read the Mission #10 file to your class. **Our mission is to study the lives of James in the Bible and Jim Elliot. Find out why <u>some missionaries might give their lives so others can hear about God</u>.**

ALL ABOARD FOR BIBLE TRUTH   Various Scriptures
(Bible Discover and Learn Time)

■ **Objective:** *The children will study Matthew 4:18–22; Mark 3:13–19; 6:19–20; John 18:1–11; 21:1–14; Acts 2:1–13; 2:42–47; 8:1–3; 12:1–2 to understand why people might willingly sacrifice their own lives so others could hear about God.*
■ **Materials:** *paper strips of stories of James and Jim Elliot, "James" and "Jim" pushpins, extra pushpins, world map*

Today, everyone will help tell the stories of James and Jim Elliot! Divide the class into two groups, balancing older and younger children. Have a helper take one group and you'll take the other group. Give your helper story strips 1–6 of James's story. Your group will use strips 1–6 of Jim Elliot's story. *You should keep strip 7 of each story apart.*

In groups, distribute the story strips. Then, rehearse how to share the story aloud, e.g. you might have children read the story strips aloud dramatically while other group members add sound effects. Encourage children to think about what they believe their missionary did when faced with the hard choice on strip 6. After several minutes preparation, allow groups to take turns using their story strips to present the stories.

James' Story

1. Jesus asked men to follow Him. James and John, sons of Zebedee, were in their fishing boat with their father. Jesus called to them to follow Him. They got right out of the boat, left their work, and became friends of Jesus. They were Jesus' disciples.
2. James was with Jesus when Roman soldiers came to arrest Him.
3. After Jesus' death and resurrection, Jesus appeared to James and six other disciples while they were fishing. Jesus made them breakfast on the beach.
4. James was watching when Jesus was taken up into heaven to sit at the right hand of God.
5. James was part of the first church where everybody shared with each other. A lot of people were excited to hear more about Jesus, and many people became Christians.
6. That made the city leaders angry. They decided to get rid of the Christians. People had to hide or run away to another city, or they would be put in jail or killed.
7. *(Hold aside until after discission below.)* King Herod had James arrested, and James was put to death by the sword.

After story strip 6, ask the class: **What choices did James have?** (James could run away, be silent, and live a peaceful life, or he could choose to stay and continue to teach and risk getting into trouble) **What would you choose? What do you think he chose?** Hand story strip 7 to the StationMaster to read aloud. **Why would James choose this?** Acknowledge children's responses. **He knew he would go to heaven. For him, to have people hear about Jesus was more important than any possible consequence.**

Now let's hear the story of Jim Elliot. Have the Jim Elliot group share their story.

Jim Elliot's Story

1. Jim Elliot grew up in Portland, Oregon in the 1940's. He loved to spend weeks at a time camping and fishing in the woods with his brothers.
2. Jim knew God wanted him to tell others about Jesus. He studied hard in college and then learned how to speak a different language and write it down. He wanted to write down the Bible for people who had never heard it before.
3. God told Jim to go to Ecuador in South America with four other men. They wanted to tell the Auca Indians about God's love for them. Nobody before had ever wanted to go near the Aucas because they were a mean, dangerous tribe.
4. Jim and the four missionary men prayed for the Aucas. They used a small plane to go to the jungle where the Aucas lived. They dropped gifts from the airplane into the villages so the Aucas would know they were friendly.
5. The five missionaries set up camp in the middle of Auca territory. They hoped some of the Aucas would come talk with them. They made sure to bring their guns because there were dangerous animals in the Amazon jungle.

6. Three Auca Indians came and spoke with them. Jim and the other missionaries were so excited! After spending the day together, the three Aucas left. Nobody came the next day. The following day, though, Auca warriors attacked the missionaries' camp.

7. *(Hold aside until after discission below.)* As Jim and his friends tried to tell the warriors about Jesus, they were killed. All five men were killed by Indian spears.

After story strip 6, again ask: **What do you think happened next? What choices did Jim Elliot and his friends have?** Help children decide that they could fight back to save their own lives, because they did have guns. Or they could keep trying to tell the warriors about a loving God. **What do you think that Jim and the other men chose to do?** Read story strip 7 aloud.

The Auca Indians did not know God. More than anything else, Jim Elliott and his missionary friends wanted to tell them about a God who loved them. They would not kill the Indians.

These are both sad stories, aren't they? But there is a happy ending! Because James didn't give up, more people heard the good new about Jesus. James did not let fear keep him from doing the work God gave him to do.

Jim Elliot and the other missionaries gave up their lives so others would hear about Jesus. And today many Auca people are Christians because of Jim and the other men. <u>Some missionaries give their lives so others can hear about God</u>.

Let's put James and Jim Elliot on our map. Place the "James" pushpin by the Sea of Galilee. **He was killed in Jerusalem for telling others about Jesus.** Stick a tack in Jerusalem. Draw a line between the tacks.

Jim Elliot grew up in Portland, Oregon. Place the "Jim" pushpin in Portland, Oregon. **Jim Elliot was called by God to be a missionary to the Auca Indians in Ecuador.** Stick a tack in Ecuador. Draw a line between the tacks.

Use the Clues!
(Bible Review)
- ■ *Materials: Mission Passcard sets, Mission Passcard #10*
Hand out Mission Passcard rings and Mission Passcard #10. Then begin asking some review questions:
- ■ **How did James know about Jesus?** (James was a close friend and disciple to Jesus and was with him when he was arrested, died and went back to heaven)
- ■ **Why did James choose to keep talking about Jesus, even when Christians were being hurt and arrested?** (he knew sharing God with others was more important than what might happen to him)
- ■ **What did James give up so that others** could hear about Jesus? (his life)
- ■ **Why did Jim Elliot go to Ecuador?** (he wanted to tell people who hadn't heard of God that Jesus loved them)
- ■ **What did Jim Elliot give up so the Aucas could understand that God loved them?** (his life)
- ■ **What happened to the Auca Indians because Jim Elliot and the other four missionaries gave their lives?** (many of the Aucas heard about Jesus)

Choose a few older children to ask one question each from their card sets, and allow the rest of the class to raise their hand if they can answer. Children can use their cards to find answers. *Helpers should collect card sets for use next week.*

BIBLE MEMORY WAYPOINT   Joshua 1:9

- **Objective:** *Children will hide God's Word in their hearts for guidance, protection, and encouragement.*

Be <u>strong</u> and courageous. Do not be <u>terrified</u>; do not be discouraged, for the Lord your God will be with <u>you</u> wherever you go (Joshua 1:9).

As you teach today's Bible memory verse phrase by phrase, demonstrate the ASL motions and have children do the motions with you. You can learn the signs for these words at these websites:
- http://commtechlab.msu.edu/sites/aslweb/browser.htm
- http://www.lifeprint.com

If you choose, delegate the teaching of the memory verse to a helper who will learn the ASL signs and teach them weekly. Ask some volunteers to join you in teaching the verse and signs to the class.

PRAYER STATION

- **Objective:** *Children will explore and practice prayer for themselves in small groups.*
- **Materials:** *Copies of* StationMaster Card #10 *for each helper*

Break into small groups of three to five children. Assign a teen or adult helper to each small group and give each helper a copy of *StationMaster Card #10* (see Resources, 95) with ideas for group discussion and prayer.

SNACK STOP: ECUADORIAN FRUIT FEST (Optional)

If you plan to provide a snack, this is an ideal time to serve it.

- **Materials:** *bananas, watermelon, pineapple, papaya—all cut in bite-size pieces, toothpicks*

Ecuador where Jim Elliot went as a missionary to the Aucas has lots of fresh fruits. They have fruit we've never heard of in our country! But these are ones we've had before. Serve platters of the fruit and give each child a toothpick to use to spear fruit bites.

Note: Always be aware of children with food allergies and have another option on hand if necessary.

APPLICATION

■ *Objective: Children will have opportunities to show how the lesson works in their own lives through activities and take-home papers.*

Some children's ministries may allow children to play outside at this point. If yours does not, choose one of the following activities.

Mosaic Parrot

■ *Materials: enlarged copies of parrot page, pre-cut colored paper bits, glue sticks*

Ecuador's tropical rainforests have lots of cool animals and birds, including parrots. Hand out copies of the parrot line art. Applying glue to one area of the parrot at a time, children can stick on different colors of paper squares to create a colorful Ecuadorian rainforest parrot. They can tear the squares into triangles or rectangles as needed.

Missionary Relay

■ *Materials: Missionary Kit (see Get Set)*

Divide the class into two or more teams. For each team, assemble a missionary kit (as identical as possible). Put the kit items in a suitcase, duffle bag or other travel type bag. Teams will line up at one end of the room. At your signal, the first player in each team takes one item from the missionary kit and puts it on, then races to the far end and back. He keeps the item as he goes to the back of the line. Once he returns to the team and tags the next player, that person takes another item from the kit, puts it on and races down to the end and back. Continue until all team members have had a turn.

ON THE FAST TRACK! *(Take-home Papers)*

Award trips to the treasure box for children who brought back a signed ticket. Give each child an *On the Fast Track!* paper. **Each week you can take home an *On the Fast Track!* paper and do the activities and practice the memory verse. When you've done those things, ask a parent to sign the ticket** (point it out). **Bring back the ticket and you can take a trip into the treasure box** (hold up box).

   Now, who wants take home *On the Fast Track?* Get children excited about doing the weekly activities.

   Hand out the children's mosaic parrots if they made them.

LESSON ELEVEN: Training Before Serving

Memory Verse:
<u>Train</u> yourself to be <u>godly</u> (1 Timothy 4:7).

Bible Basis:
2 Timothy 2:1–7

Bible Truth:
Missionaries train to serve God well.

Timothy · Hudson Taylor

You Will Need:

- [ ] pushpins
- [ ] cardstock or stiff paper
- [ ] 1 poster board
- [ ] Mission Files
- [ ] Mission Passcard #11
- [ ] rings with Mission Passcard sets
- [ ] world map
- [ ] masking tape
- [ ] CD/tape player and music
- [ ] cardboard or poster board
- [ ] origami paper for each child (or cut wrapping paper into 6" squares)
- [ ] origami instructions (You can find instructions online by doing a web search of "easy+origami+instructions")
- [ ] *On the Fast Track! #11* take-home paper
- [ ] *StationMaster Card #11*
- [ ] *(Optional)* treasure box
- [ ] *(Optional)* Snack: pineapple cubes and/or pear slices, toothpicks
- [ ] *(Optional)* Activity #2: red tempera paint, clean Styrofoam meat trays, craft brushes, half a potato for each child, white paper, plastic knives, small cookie cutters

 When you see this icon, it means preparation will take more than five minutes.

 GET SET!
(Lesson Preparation)

- ▪ Make a copy of *On the Fast Track! #11* take-home paper for each child.
- ▪ Make a copy of *StationMaster Card #11* for each helper.
- ▪ Photocopy, fold, and hole punch Mission Passcard #11 on cardstock or stiff paper for each child.
- ▪ Cut one quarter-sized circle out of cardstock. Write the name "Hudson Taylor" on it.
- ▪ Copy an origami pattern and instructions for each helper, if using the Welcome Time Activity.
- ▪ Create a masking tape square, rectangle, or circle on the floor, large enough for all the children to stand on without being crowded. Make a large "X" with permanent marker on one section of tape.
- ▪ Draw and cut out several cardboard or poster board templates in oval, square, and rectangular shapes. The templates should be about 3–4" wide.
- ▪ Arrange with a StationMaster helper to bring in the Mission Files with urgency and drama during the Sharing Time today and following weeks.
- ▪ Print this week's memory verse on the poster board.

 TICKETS PLEASE!
(Welcome and Bible Connection)

- ▪ **Objective:** *To excite children's interest and connect training to the Bible Truth, children will learn how to make an origami figure.*

Welcome Time Activity: Learning Lab

■ *Materials: colored paper, origami pattern*

As children arrive, direct them to the table where helpers are waiting to work with a few children at a time. The helpers will teach the children to make a simple origami folded design. Helpers can engage children in conversation about other things they've learned, such as how to whistle, ride a bike, or do a craft. When everyone has arrived, call the children to the lesson area.

Sharing Time and Bible Connection

Introduce today's lesson by discussing the following questions. As you talk, give every child the opportunity to say something.

■ **How many of you learned something new by doing the origami activity?**
■ **Who here has learned or is learning how to read?** Affirm show of hands.
■ **What are some of the things you still need to learn?**

After discussion time, help your students connect their discussion to the Bible story they are about to hear from 2 Timothy 2:1–7. Signal the helper waiting outside to hurry in urgently and hand you the Mission Files. The helper should say with drama: **You've been given a mission!** Say: **Another mission, yes! Let's see what our assignment is for today.** Take out the Mission #11 file from the Mission Files and read it to your class. **To complete our mission today, we need to study the lives of two people—Timothy and Hudson Taylor. We need to find out if <u>missionaries do training</u>.**

 # ALL ABOARD FOR BIBLE TRUTH   2 Timothy 2:1-7
(Bible Discover and Learn Time)

■ *Objective: The children will study 2 Timothy 2:1–7 and explore the training of Timothy and Hudson Taylor to understand why missionaries undergo training.*
■ *Materials: "Hudson" pushpin, extra pushpins, world map*

Divide the class into two groups. One will be the soldiers, the other the athletes. Assign a helper to each group and have the groups huddle to decide what kind of training their athletes (or soldiers) would need to be very good at their work. Helpers should help the group plan a demonstration of their training ideas. After a couple of minutes preparation, invite groups to sit and hear about Timothy.

Who remembers what we learned about the New Testament missionary named Timothy? He traveled with Paul as a missionary, Paul called him a brother and fellow worker, Timothy did the work of a pastor when Paul couldn't come with him. **You're right. We can learn from Timothy's life another important fact about missionaries.**

Paul was an experienced missionary when he started working with Timothy. Timothy was a young man who didn't know what to expect or how to do the work. So Paul had to train and teach him. But it wasn't like going to school, with books and tests. Paul told Timothy that he needed to prepare for missionary work like a soldier prepares for battle. Ask the soldier group to demonstrate their training ideas.

Thanks for those good ideas about how soldiers train. Paul wrote to Timothy that he should expect to endure hardship like a good soldier of Jesus Christ. Soldiers have to sometimes walk long distances carrying heavy packs. They might have to sleep in unusual places and eat food that isn't their favorite. But they do these things willingly because they want to become the best soldiers they can.

Paul reminded Timothy that a soldiers in the army needs to keep his mind on his job, and not get distracted by anything else. A soldier has to concentrate on obeying the commander in charge.

Ask the athlete group to demonstrate their training ideas. **Thanks for those great examples of how athletes train. Paul also told Timothy that he needed to prepare to be a missionary like an athlete prepares for a contest. He said no athlete ever won a competition without following the rules. And that means they have to train hard and faithfully. If you play a sport, you know you have to learn game rules really well and practice to be good at it.**

Now Paul wasn't trying to train Timothy to become a soldier or a ball player. He was showing Timothy that being a missionary was so important, it was worth the work to learn to do it well. Timothy needed to learn how to tell people about Jesus. He had to stick with the work even when it was hard or he felt tired. Good soldiers and athletes can't give up when they're tired or frustrated. Missionaries can't either. Missionaries learn to live in the country where God sends them. They might have to learn a new language, learn different ways to travel, and learn how to live like the people in the foreign country.

Hudson Taylor is another missionary who understood how important it was to be trained to do missionary work. Hudson lived over 100 years ago. He grew up in England. As a young man like Timothy, he realized God wanted him to tell people in China who Jesus is. Hudson knew he needed training. He studied medicine so he could be a doctor to the Chinese people. But that wasn't all. Hudson also studied the Bible and spent lots of time getting to know God very well. Hudson learned to trust in God very much.

When he got to China, Hudson practiced speaking in Chinese. He also learned how the Chinese people dressed and lived, and he did his best to live like they did. Hudson Taylor spread the news of Jesus in China and invited many more missionaries to join him in China. Chinese people today are learning about Jesus because Hudson Taylor trained and went there as a missionary. Both Timothy and Hudson Taylor trained hard to be good missionaries and God used them both in a big way. Even if we aren't training

to be missionaries right now, God still wants us to train like soldiers to serve Him—to study our Bibles, learn about Him, and get strong in our faith.

We already have Timothy on the map. Where did he start working with Paul? Lystra. **Point to the "Timothy" pushpin in central Turkey)**

Hudson Taylor grew up in Yorkshire, England. Place the "Hudson" pushpin in England. **He served God as a missionary in China.** Stick a pin on the Chinese coast. Draw a line from Hudson to the pin in China.

Use the Clues!
(Bible Review)
- **Materials:** *masking tape line, music, Mission Passcard sets, Mission Passcard #11*

Have helpers hand out Mission Passcard rings. Then, hand out Mission Readiness Card #11 which children will place on their rings behind card #10. Have children take a place on the masking tape line. As you play music, they'll march around on the line. When you stop the music, everyone stops. The child standing on or nearest the "X" has a chance to answer a review question. Start with today's questions, then ask several from previous lessons using the Mission Passcard rings.

- **What two examples of training did Paul tell Timothy about?** (a soldier, an athlete)
- **Why did Timothy need to be trained as a missionary?** (so he could endure hardship, know how to tell people about Jesus, stick with the work when he was tired or frustrated)
- **How did Hudson Taylor train for missionary work?** (he learned about medicine, studied the Bible, learned to speak Chinese, learned how the Chinese people lived)
- **What difference did Hudson Taylor make in China?** (he started the missionary work there and because of him more missionaries came to China to share Jesus.) *After the game, collect the card rings.*

BIBLE MEMORY WAYPOINT   1 Timothy 4:7

- *Objective: Children will hide God's Word in their hearts for guidance, protection, and encouragement.*

Train yourself to be godly (1 Timothy 4:7).

As you teach today's Bible memory verse phrase by phrase, demonstrate the ASL motions and have children do the motions with you. You can learn the signs for these words at these websites:
- **http://commtechlab.msu.edu/sites/aslweb/browser.htm**
- **http://www.lifeprint.com**

If you choose, delegate the teaching of the memory verse to a helper who will learn the ASL signs and teach them weekly. As you go over this memory verse, have children do jumping jacks in rhythm with the words, stopping on the underlined words. Explain that training is often tiring, just like jumping makes them feel after a while. Encourage them to continue jumping until everyone has learned the memory verse.

PRAYER STATION

- ■ *Objective:* Children will explore and practice prayer for themselves in small groups.
- ■ *Materials:* Copies of StationMaster Card #11 for each helper

Break into small groups of three to five children. Assign a teen or adult helper to each small group and give each helper a copy of *StationMaster Card #11* (see Resources, 95) with ideas for group discussion and prayer.

SNACK STOP: FRESH FRUIT, CHINESE STYLE (Optional)

If you plan to provide a snack, this is an ideal time to serve it.

- ■ *Materials:* fresh pear slices or pineapple cubes, toothpicks

Chinese people enjoy fresh fruit. They have some fruits we've never heard of, but they also eat fruit like pineapple and pears. Many of their snacks are on sticks, so we have fruit on toothpicks to remind us how the Chinese eat their snacks. Let children help themselves to fruit on toothpicks.

APPLICATION

- ■ *Objective:* Children will have opportunities to show how the lesson works in their own lives through activities and take-home papers.

Some children's ministries may allow children to play outside at this point. If yours does not, choose one of the following activities.

Watch and Learn

Explain that often we learn new things by watching others do them and following their example. This game requires children to imitate actions you or a helper demonstrate. Start with simple actions, like toe touches, various handclap sequences, jumping and hopping. Progress to more challenging actions, such as a series of three moves that the children watch, then perform. After you've led some actions, invite a volunteer to try being the leader.

 ## Chinese Chops

■ *Materials: red tempera paint, clean Styrofoam meat trays, craft brushes, half a potato for each child, white paper, plastic knives, small cookie cutters*

You can learn about authentic Chinese chops (seals) online. Try doing a websearch on the words "Chinese+chop+seals."

Tell the children that they're going to make a Chinese chop. Explain that a chop is like a personal seal that has their name or a personal design on it. Chinese people use a chop to sign a piece of art work or important document. Hand out half a potato and a plastic knife to each child. Put cookie cutters within reach of everyone.

Have children press a cookie cutter shape deeply into the flat surface of the potato. With a plastic knife, cut the outside edge of the potato away from the design. When finished, pour a small amount of red tempera paint on the Styrofoam trays and place them where everyone can reach. Children will brush red paint on the design surface of the potato and "stamp" the design onto white paper.

 ## ON THE FAST TRACK! *(Take-home Papers)*

(Optional) treasure box. Award trips to the treasure box for children who brought back a signed ticket. Hand out the *On the Fast Track!* papers and encourage children to do the work and learn the verse at home. **When you take your *On the Fast Track!* paper home, you can do the activities and learn the verse. Then ask a parent to sign the ticket. When you bring the ticket back next week, you'll get a prize from the treasure box.**

Before they leave, give children their Chinese chop prints if they made them.

LESSON TWELVE: Far From Home

Titus · Church Missionary

Memory Verse:
Let your light <u>shine</u> before men, that they may <u>see</u> your good deeds, and praise your <u>Father</u> in <u>heaven</u> (Matthew 5:16).

Bible Basis:
The Book of Titus

Bible Truth:
Some missionaries spend many years in a foreign country.

You Will Need:

- [ ] pushpins
- [ ] cardstock or stiff paper
- [ ] 1 poster board
- [ ] Mission Files
- [ ] Mission Passcard #12
- [ ] rings with Mission Passcard sets
- [ ] world map
- [ ] paper cups
- [ ] *(Optional)* TV and VCR
- [ ] *On the Fast Track! #12*
- [ ] *StationMaster Card #12*
- [ ] *(Optional)* treasure box
- [ ] *(Optional)* Snack: pita chips or rice crackers, dried mango or pineapple pieces, napkins, cups
- [ ] *(Optional)* Activity #1: blocks and other building materials, such as empty boxes, pillows, etc.
- [ ] *(Optional)* Activity #2: play dough (see recipe, p. 30), cardboard squares, book or picture showing an amphora (urn). You can find pictures online by doing a web search of "Greek+amphora."

When you see this icon, it means preparation will take more than five minutes.

GET SET!
(Lesson Preparation)

- ■ Make a copy of *On the Fast Track! #12* take-home paper for each child.
- ■ Make a copy of *StationMaster Card #12* for each helper.
- ■ Photocopy, fold, and hole punch Mission Passcard #12 on cardstock or stiff paper for each child. Write the name of your church-sponsored missionary on it.
- ■ Cut quarter-sized circles out of cardstock. Write the name "Titus" on one circle and the name of your *church-sponsored missionary family* on the other. Glue each circle to the head of a pushpin.
- ■ Follow-up with the *church-sponsored missionary family* and/or find the materials they sent you.
- ■ Arrange with a StationMaster helper to bring in the Mission Files with urgency and drama during the Sharing Time today.
- ■ Print this week's memory verse on the poster board.

TICKETS PLEASE!
(Welcome and Bible Connection)

- ■ **Objective:** *To excite children's interest and connect the different ways to tell others about Jesus to the Bible Truth, children will play a cooperative game.*

Welcome Time Activity: God Loves You!

■ *Materials: construction paper in assorted colors, cut sheets into fourths, scissors, markers, round objects to trace*

As children arrive, have them make "God Loves You" buttons to trade. Write the words "God Loves You" on the whiteboard. Let children trace circles on construction paper, cut them out, and copy the words in the center. Then decorate the button with markers. As soon as they make one, they should give it to someone in the room. If they receive a button from someone, they should give it to another child. As they pass a button to someone, they should say, "God loves you." Children should be passing buttons to each other or making new buttons. When everyone has arrived, call the children to the lesson area.

Sharing Time and Bible Connection

Introduce today's lesson by discussing the following questions with your students in the large group. As you talk, give every child the opportunity to say something.

■ **How long do you think you'll live at home with your families?**
■ **Why do you think children live at home so long before they move to their own home and live on their own**? (because they need to grow up and learn many things, they're learning about life from their families)
■ **How long do you imagine a missionary might need to stay in another country to share about Jesus?** Let children share their ideas.
■ **Many missionaries stay in the country where they're sharing Jesus for a long time. They live there like it's their new home. Teaching people to grow in their faith in God can take a long time.**

After discussion time, help your students connect their discussion to the Bible story they are about to hear from the book of Titus. Signal the helper waiting outside to hurry in urgently and hand you the Mission Files. The helper should say with drama: **You've been given a mission!** Say: **Another mission! After today, we only have one week left in our study of missionaries. Let's see what our assignment is for today.** Ask a volunteer to take out Mission #12 from the Mission Files and read it aloud. **To complete our mission today, we need to investigate the lives of Titus and** (church-sponsored missionary family's name)**. We need to find out why some missionaries spend many years in a foreign country.**

ALL ABOARD FOR BIBLE TRUTH   Book of Titus
(Bible Discover and Learn Time)

- **Objective:** *The children will delve into the book of Titus to understand how some missionaries, like Titus and* (church sponsored missionary family's name), *leave their homes for a long time to live with people who don't know Jesus.*
- **Materials:** *Paper cups, writing paper, pens, markers, TV and VCR (optional), world map, "Titus" and "church-sponsored missionary" pushpins; extra pushpins*

Raise your hand if you live in a community. Let children respond. **Tell me about some of the communities of which you are a part.** (family, school, neighborhood) **What is a community?** (a group of people who share something) **Is your church a community? Yes! What do we share?** (We share a belief in and love for God) **It can take a long time for a community to grow strong together. Sometimes it takes a whole lifetime!**

Do you remember Paul? Let children answer. **He was one of the first missionaries we've talked about. Paul and another believer named Titus traveled together. They went to an island called Crete to tell as many people as they could about Jesus. They wanted to grow a new community. This new community was made of people who loved God and were obedient to Him. It was a church! Let's use cups to show this community.** Choose volunteers to set up three rows of 6 cups, upside down on the floor.

That's what Paul and Titus did. They told the people of Crete that God loved them. They lived with the people and taught them how to live God's way. Paul and Titus also corrected their mistakes so they would grow strong. Then Paul left Crete to tell other people about God's love.

But Titus stayed! Titus stayed on Crete to help the new believers build their community of faith. Paul had told Titus how the people in charge of the churches in Crete should act. And Titus made sure the people of Crete understood what God

had wanted them to do. Ask volunteers to place two rows of cups (upside down) on the three rows of cups that are already on the floor. **The church grew!**

Titus stayed to teach the people of Crete how God wanted them to live. They learned how to be kind and how to devote themselves to what was right and what pleased God. The believers grew some more! Ask volunteers to place one row of cups (upside down) on the two rows of cups. **That's what some missionaries do. They stay for a long time with the same people to teach them how to be closer to God.**

Now let's meet the (church-sponsored missionary family's name) **family. They chose to leave their home in** (city or state where they originally lived) **and moved to** (place where they live now) **to tell others about Jesus.**

Read their letter and/or show their video to your class. **The** (church-sponsored missionary family's name) **family is doing a lot to help others know about God.** Describe the work the missionaries are involved in. Have volunteers continue to stack individual cups on the previous row of cups. **Let's see how high you can make it.** Continue until cups are about to fall, then stop.

Look at how our structure has grown! This is a picture of how people can grow

to know Jesus when missionaries stay with them and help them. When missionaries spend their their lives teaching the people about God, their faith gets stronger and bigger.

The *(church-sponsored missionary family's name)* **family wrote a letter to us, so now we're going to write letters to them. It's pretty lonely sometimes to be away from all their family and friends. You can tell them thank you for telling others about Jesus. You can tell them they're doing a good job and you will pray for them. Tell them something about yourself and what you've learned about missionaries.** Hand out paper. Write the family's name on the board. StationMasters may assist children where needed or encourage them to draw a picture for the family. Allow up to 15 minutes to produce the letters.

NOTE: If the missionary family is serving in a region where the government may be hostile to Christian missionaries, help the children avoid potentially sensitive language or topics.

Great job! Let's see where Titus and this missionary family are in the world. Titus probably started in Jerusalem with Paul. Place the "Titus" pushpin in Jerusalem. Titus and Paul traveled to the island of Crete. **Titus stayed on Crete to help the church grow in their faith in God.** Stick another pin on the island of Crete. With a marker, draw a line between the two tacks.

(Church-sponsored missionary family's name) **started in** *(city where they lived)*. Place the pushpin with their name at that location. **They traveled to** *(place where they live now)* **to live with the people there.** Stick a pin at that location. Draw a line between the two tacks.

I know your letters will bless the *(church-sponsored missionary family's name)*. **Even though they're far away in** *(location)* **to share Jesus with people there, we can pray for them over here.**

BIBLE MEMORY WAYPOINT

Matthew 5:16

Use the Clues!
(Bible Review)

■ *Materials: Mission Passcard sets, Mission Passcard #12*

Helpers hand out Mission Passcard rings. Then hand out Mission Passcard #12 and let children place it behind Passcard #11. Read it together briefly, then ask some review questions from today's lesson.

■ **How did Titus helped build a strong community of believers on Crete?** (he stayed with them to help grow their faith, teach them, encourage them, and show them God's ways)

■ **How have** *(church-sponsored missionary family's name)* **helped the people in** *(location)* **make a strong foundation in their faith in Jesus?**

■ **Why do many missionaries stay for a long time with people in a faraway place?** (to be sure the Christians are growing in their faith and learning how to live God's way)

Continue the review of previous lessons by letting children divide up into pairs and quiz each other for several minutes using the Passcards. *When finished, helpers should collect card sets for use next week.*

BIBLE MEMORY WAYPOINT   Matthew 5:16

- *Objective: Children will hide God's Word in their hearts for guidance, protection, and encouragement.*

Let your light <u>shine</u> before men, that they may <u>see</u> your good deeds, and praise your <u>Father</u> in <u>heaven</u> (Matthew 5:16).

As you teach today's Bible memory verse phrase by phrase, demonstrate the ASL motions for the underlined words and have children do the motions with you. You can learn the signs for these words at these websites:

- **http://commtechlab.msu.edu/sites/aslweb/browser.htm**
- **http://www.lifeprint.com**

If you choose, delegate the teaching of the memory verse to a helper who will learn the ASL signs and teach them weekly.

To make memorizing more fun, divide the girls to one side of the room and the boys to the other. Begin by having the girls recite the words of the verse while the boys fill in with the signs. Do this a couple of times, and then switch jobs.

PRAYER STATION

- *Objective: Children will explore and practice prayer for themselves in small groups.*
- *Materials: Copies of StationMaster Card #12 for each helper*

Break into small groups of three to five children. Assign a teen or adult helper to each small group and give each helper a copy of *StationMaster Card #12* (see Resources, 96) with ideas for group discussion and prayer.

SNACK STOP: NEW TASTES

If you plan to provide a snack, this is an ideal time to serve it.

- *Materials: Pita chips or rice crackers, dried mango or pineapple pieces, napkins, cups*

When the missionaries move to a different place to live, they have to get used to a lot of new things. They learn to eat new kinds of food. So today we're going to try some new things. Hand out snacks and identify them, and serve cups of water. Discuss the other adaptations missionaries might make in a foreign location.

Note: Be aware of children with food allergies and have another option on hand.

APPLICATION

■ *Objective: Children will have opportunities to show how the lesson works in their own lives through activities and take-home papers.*

Some children's ministries may allow children to play outside at this point. If yours does not, choose one of the following activities.

House Building Challenge

■ *Materials: blocks and other building materials, such as empty boxes, pillows, etc.*

Brainstorm the types of houses people live in, in other parts of the world (igloo, hut, cave, adobe brick, lean-to, apartment, teepee). After exhausting the children's ideas (and your own), divide the class into five groups. Assign each group one of the home styles, asking them to cooperatively construct it using whatever materials you provide. After the groups are finished or you call time, have each group present their home. Talk for a few minutes about how life would be different if the children lived in the house they built. Remind them that missionaries who live in foreign places often have homes very different from what we know.

Greek Amphora

■ *Materials: play dough, book or picture showing an amphora (urn), cardboard squares*

Tell children that Crete is part of the country of Greece in the southern part of Europe. People have lived there for thousands of years. The people used to make urns called amphorae to carry water and hold oil and wine. Show the picture and let children form their own amphora from clay or play dough. Place each creation on a cardboard square to take home.

ON THE FAST TRACK! *(Take-home Papers)*

Award trips to the treasure box for children who brought back a signed ticket. Hand out the *On the Fast Track!* papers and encourage children to do the work and learn the verse at home. **When you take your *On the Fast Track!* paper home, you can do the activities and learn the verse. Then ask a parent to sign the ticket. When you bring the ticket back next week, you'll get a prize from the treasure box.**

Now, who wants take home *On the Fast Track?* Get children excited about doing the weekly activities.

Hand out amphorae to take home as children leave.

Memory Verse:

Then I <u>heard</u> the voice of the <u>Lord</u> saying, "Whom shall I <u>send</u>? And who will go for us?" And I said, "Here am <u>I</u>. <u>Send</u> me!" (Isaiah 6:8).

Bible Truth:

You and I can be missionaries.

Bible Basis:

Deuteronomy 10:19a;
1 Chronicles 16:23–24;
Psalm 9:11; 67:1–2; 96:3, 10; 105:1;
Isaiah 12:4–5; Isaiah 49:6b;
Matthew 9:37-38; 24:14; Mark 13:10; 16:15;
Romans 10:14; 2 Corinthians 5:20; 1 Timothy 2:3–4; 2 Timothy 4:2

You Will Need:

- [ ] pushpins
- [ ] cardstock or stiff paper
- [ ] 1 poster board
- [ ] Mission Files
- [ ] Mission Passcard #13
- [ ] rings with Mission Passcard sets
- [ ] world map
- [ ] Bibles
- [ ] wooden or plastic hoop, about 18" across
- [ ] several jigsaw puzzles
- [ ] construction paper in a variety of colors
- [ ] *On the Fast Track!* #13 take-home paper
- [ ] *StationMaster Card #13*
- [ ] (Optional) treasure box
- [ ] (Optional) Snack: bugle-shaped crackers, water, cups, napkins
- [ ] (Optional) Activity #1: CD/tape player, praise music
- [ ] (Optional) Activity #2: pre-screened collection of travel or geographic magazines; large white construction paper; markers or crayons, glitter glue, variety of stickers, crayons or markers

 When you see this icon, preparation will take more than five minutes.

GET SET!
(Lesson Preparation)

- ▪ Make a copy of *On the Fast Track! #13* take-home paper for each child.
- ▪ Make a copy of *StationMaster Card #13* for each helper.
- ▪ Photocopy, fold, and hole punch Mission Passcard #13 on cardstock or stiff paper for each child.
- ▪ ⏰ Cut a 2" circle out of cardstock. Write the word "YOU" in fancy letters on the circle. Tape the circle to the head of a pushpin.
- ▪ Cut construction paper into 3" x 11" strips, Write one reference on each strip: Deuteronomy 10:19a; 1 Chronicles 16:23-24; Psalm 9:11; Psalm 67:1-2; Psalm 96:3; Psalm 96:10; Psalm 105:1; Isaiah 12:4; Isaiah 12:5; Isaiah 49:6b; Matthew 9:37-38; Matthew 24:14; Mark 13:10; Mark 16:15; Romans 10:14; 2 Corinthians 5:20; 1 Timothy 2:3-4; 2 Timothy 4:2.
- ▪ Set the puzzles in different areas on the floor.
- ▪ Arrange with a StationMaster helper to bring in the Mission Files with drama during Sharing Time.
- ▪ ⏰ Print this week's memory verse on the poster board.

TICKETS PLEASE!
(Welcome and Bible Connection)

■ **Objective:** *To excite children's interest and connect all the previous lessons in this unit to today's Bible Truth, children will work with puzzles.*

Welcome Time Activity: Puzzle Time

■ **Materials:** *several jigsaw puzzles, appropriate for all age groups (remove one piece from each puzzle)*

As children arrive, direct them to the helper at the front of the classroom. Around the helper will be many puzzles. All the helpers can work with the children on the puzzles. As children finish the puzzles, they'll find one piece missing out of each. Helpers can engage children in conversation about why there are pieces missing. When everyone has arrived, call the children to the lesson area. Keep the puzzles intact for later use.

Sharing Time and Bible Connection

Introduce today's lesson by discussing the following questions. As you talk, give every child the opportunity to say something.

■ **How did your puzzle-making activity turn out?** (a piece was missing)
■ **Today we're going to talk about a piece of the missions puzzle. We've learned about a lot of missionaries and how they work and why they do it. This last lesson will show us what that missing piece is.**

After discussion time, signal the helper waiting outside to come in and hand you the Mission Files. The helper should say with drama: **This is your last mission.**
 Can you believe this is our last week? What have we learned about being an effective missionary? Prompt children to name as many Bible truths as they can recall. Missionaries and lesson themes are listed below:

1. *Missionaries are people who tell others about Jesus.*
2. *God can turn unbelievers into missionaries.* (Paul and Adoniram)
3. *God gives missionaries the strength to stay, even in hard times.* (Silas and Mary)
4. *Missionaries work together to get the job done.* (Timothy and Cook Ministries)
5. *Missionaries can tell people about God in their own cities.* (Stephen and George)
6. *God loves to encourage His missionaries.* (Barnabas and Betty)
7. *Some missionaries write down God's Word for others to read.* (Luke and Cameron)
8. *Some missionaries go on short journeys.* (Philip and *short-term missionary's name*)
9. *God can do miracles as His missionaries work for Him.* (Peter and Jonathan)
10. *Some missionaries give their lives so others can hear about God.* (James and Jim Elliot)
11. *Missionaries need training to serve God well.* (Timothy and Hudson Taylor)

12. *Some missionaries spend many years in a foreign country.* (Titus and *name of church-sponsored missionary family*)
Continue with the responses until all of the children have been allowed to share.

Wow! We've learned a lot about what makes a great missionary. But just who can be a missionary? The Bible answers this question for us.

ALL ABOARD FOR BIBLE TRUTH   **Various Scriptures**
(Bible Discover and Learn Time)

- **Objective:** *The children will study Bible passages to understand what makes a good missionary.*
- **Materials:** *various colors of construction paper strips, markers, stapler, Bibles, wooden or plastic hoop at least 18" in diameter, Bibles*

Hand out one strip of construction paper with a verse on it to pairs of students (pair older and younger children). Each pair will need a marker and a Bible. Pairs will look up their verse in the Bible, with assistance from helpers as needed. After each pair has found and read through their verse, bring the children back together.
I'm going to have each of you read your verse for the class. After you read it, you'll staple your strip of paper to this hoop. Let each pair read their verse, then help them loop their paper strip through onto the hoop and staple it. When you have four loops on the hoop, link all remaining paper strips off those four loops, making chains. You'll have four chains in all, attached to the hoop.
What did all these verses tell us about being a missionary? Let children respond. **We can all be missionaries. You and I can all tell others about Jesus in our own neighborhoods or across the world.**
Point to the world map where you have followed the lives of missionaries. **Some missionaries stayed where they had always lived. Others went far away. If we're listening to what God wants us to do, just like He did for these missionaries, He'll show us who to talk to!**
Hold up the hoop. **The hoop is a picture of how when God sends us share about Jesus with others, His love can travel far away. Lay the hoop up against the center of the map.** Have four children hold each of the chains out to the sides, top and bottom (like compass points) to illustrate. **God can use you and me to spread His good news.**
Even though the missionaries we learned about these last months lived in different places and times, they all have something in common. What's the same about all the missionaries? Let the children respond: They all wanted other people to know what Jesus had done for them.
God gave each missionary the desire to share about Him. He sent them where He knew people were waiting to hear. God will put that same desire in the hearts of everyone in this room. The more you and I get to know God,

the more we want others to know Him too. You can share God with people in your own family, in your neighborhood, or anywhere in the world.

Hand out the missing puzzle pieces to pairs. **The missing piece of the puzzles stands for you! Each of us is part of God's plan for sharing Jesus with the world.** Let pairs fit their puzzle piece into their puzzle from the Welcome Time Activity.

Use the Clues!
(Bible Review)
■ **Materials:** *Mission Passcard sets, Mission Passcard #13*

Helpers hand out Mission Passcard rings. Then, hand out Mission Passcard #13. Check the children's understanding of today's lesson with these questions:

■ **What one thing is the same about every missionary?** (all want people to know what Jesus has done for them)

■ **How can you and I be missionaries?** (by sharing about Jesus with the people we know)

■ **Where does the desire to be a missionary come from?** (God puts it in our hearts and minds as we get to know Him better)

If time allows, review the past 12 lessons by playing the game, "Challenge." Divide the class into two teams. Teams should go into a huddle. Working together and using the Mission Passcards, each team will think of a question that will "stump" the other team. In every round, both teams have the opportunity to ask the opposing team a question. A correct answer scores one point. Repeat this process for 5 rounds. Keep score and the team with the most points at the end of 5 rounds is the winner. *Helpers should collect card sets to be handed out at the end of class to take home.*

BIBLE MEMORY WAYPOINT   Isaiah 6:8

■ *Objective: Children will hide God's Word in their hearts for guidance, protection, and encouragement.*

Then I <u>heard</u> the voice of the <u>Lord</u> saying, "Whom shall I <u>send</u>? And who will go for us?" And I said, "Here am <u>I</u>. <u>Send</u> me!" (Isaiah 6:8).

As you teach today's Bible memory verse phrase by phrase, demonstrate the ASL motions for the underlined words and have children do the motions with you. You can learn the words for each lesson at these websites:

■ **http://commtechlab.msu.edu/sites/aslweb/browser.htm**
■ **http://www.lifeprint.com**

If you choose, delegate the teaching of the memory verse to a helper who will learn the ASL signs and teach them weekly. Demonstrate the ASL motions as you teach the verse, and have children do the motions with you.

Have students form a circle around the classroom. Start by "passing" the verse to the left. The first child says the first word, the child to the left says the second word, etc. When you reach a word that will be signed, everyone should sign the word together. Continue with the next child to the left, and so on around the circle. Encourage the group to work at moving the verse around the circle smoothly. If you have a large class, you can create two groups and do the practice separately so children have more opportunity to participate.

PRAYER STATION

- ■ **Objective:** *Children will explore and practice prayer for themselves in small groups.*
- ■ **Materials:** *Copies of* StationMaster Card #13 *for each helper*

Break into small groups of three to five children. Assign a teen or adult helper to each small group and give each helper a copy of *StationMaster Card #13* (see Resources, 96) with ideas for group discussion and prayer.

SNACK STOP: MISSIONARY MUNCHIES (Optional)

If you plan to provide a snack, this is an ideal time to serve it.

- ■ **Materials:** *Bugle crackers, water, cups, napkins*

We now know that we can be missionaries, also. Telling others about Jesus is like blowing a horn to announce an important message. Pass out bugle crackers on napkins. **When you share God with others, you're planting seeds in the hearts of the people you know about who God really is.** As you pass out the cups with water, discuss how important the right attitude is when it comes to doing what God wants you to do.
Note: Always be aware of children with food allergies and have another option on hand if necessary.

APPLICATION

■ *Objective: Children will have opportunities to show how the lesson works in their own lives through activities and take-home papers.*

Some children's ministries may allow children to play outside at this point. If yours does not, choose one of the following activities.

 Praise Freeze!

■ *Materials: CD/tape player, praise CD or tape*

Play praise music for your class. Have students dance, jump, or move in any way they want. When you turn off the music, they should freeze. Anyone who moves when the music is off will sit out and join the teacher in looking for movement during the next freeze. Play until only one person is left. The game can be repeated as many times as you want.

 Where in the World? Poster

■ *Materials: pre-screened collection of travel or geographic magazines; large white construction paper; markers or crayons, glitter glue, stars and other types of stickers, crayons or markers*

Allow children to look through the magazines at world regions and talk about what they see. Encourage children to think about who God might send to bring the Gospel to these people. Lead them to understand that God can use them as missionaries at home right now, and maybe even far away, later when they're grown up. Children can create a poster for their rooms showing themselves as missionaries at home or far away. Include the title, "I Can Be a Missionary." Decorate with color, glitter, or stickers.

 ON THE FAST TRACK! *(Take-home Papers)*

(Optional) treasure box. Award trips to the treasure box for children who brought back a signed ticket. Hand out the *On the Fast Track!* papers and encourage children to do the work and learn the verse at home. **When you take your *On the Fast Track!* paper home, you can do the activities and learn the verse. Then ask a parent to sign the ticket. When you bring the ticket back next week, you can choose a prize from the treasure box.**

Before they leave, give children their own sets of Mission Passcards, and the poster if they made one.

MISSION PASSCARD 1
Identification Card

God can lead me to be a missionary.
I need to talk to Him, so he can tell me what He wants me to do.
I want everybody to know about God.

I can be a missionary!

MISSION PASSCARD 1
Identification Card

Name _____

Age _____

Color of hair _____

Color of eyes _____

MISSION PASSCARD 2
God can make unbelievers into missionaries.

Adoniram Judson (1788-1850)

■ He didn't believe in God.

■ His friend's death turned his attention toward God.

■ As a Jesus-follower, he wanted everyone to know about God.

MISSION PASSCARD 2
God can make unbelievers into missionaries.

Paul

■ He lived his own way.

■ God had to get his attention.

■ As a Jesus-follower, he wanted everyone to know about God.

MISSION PASSCARD 3
God gives missionaries strength in hard times.

Mary Slessor (1848-1915)

■ She wasn't afraid to tell others about Jesus.

■ In hard times, she kept going.

■ Because she didn't run away, more people heard about Jesus.

MISSION PASSCARD 3
God gives missionaries strength in hard times.

Silas

■ He wasn't afraid to tell others about Jesus.

■ He worshiped God in the middle of hard times.

■ Because he stayed, more people believed.

MISSION PASSCARD 4

Missionaries work together to get the job done.

Cook Communications Ministries International

- They help other missionaries, especially in developing countries.
- They help missionaries learn how to publish books about Jesus.
- They want everyone to know about God.

MISSION PASSCARD 4

Timothy

- He was a helper to Paul.
- He was willing to go wherever God sent him.
- He wanted to tell people about God.

Missionaries work together to get the job done.

MISSION PASSCARD 5

Missionaries tell people about God wherever they live.

George Mueller (1805–1898)

- He trusted God to put him in the right place to serve others.
- He took care of children in his own city.
- He wanted the children in his city to know of God's love for them.

MISSION PASSCARD 5

Stephen

- He trusted God to put him in the right place to serve others.
- He took care of people in his own city.
- He told many people in his own city about Jesus.

Missionaries tell people about God wherever they live.

MISSION PASSCARD 6

God loves to encourage his missionaries.

Betty Greene (1920–1997)

- She flew an airplane to bring missionaries things they needed.
- Her actions encouraged missionaries.
- Her help let missionaries keep teaching about Jesus.

MISSION PASSCARD 6

Barnabas

- His name means "Son of Encouragement."
- His actions encouraged others to keep going.
- He wanted to help others tell people about Jesus.

God loves to encourage his missionaries.

MISSION PASSCARD 7

Some missionaries write down God's word.

Cameron Townsend (1896-1982)

- He translated the Bible into other languages.
- He started a group that translates the Bible into other languages.
- He wanted everyone to be able to read God's Word in their own language.

MISSION PASSCARD 7

Some missionaries write down God's word.

Luke

- He wrote what God wanted him to write.
- He worked hard to make sure it was right.
- He wanted everyone to know the truth about Jesus and His resurrection.

MISSION PASSCARD 8

Some missionaries go on short journeys.

Name: _____

- This missionary followed what God asked him/her to do.
- This missionary was willing to go on a short trip.
- This missionary wanted people to know about Jesus.

MISSION PASSCARD 8

Some missionaries go on short journeys.

Philip

- He followed what God asked him to do.
- He went to different places for short times.
- He wanted people he met to know about Jesus.

MISSION PASSCARD 9

God can do miracles anytime and anyplace.

Jonathan Goforth (1859-1936)

- He was willing to go through hard times.
- God saved him with a miracle.
- He was bold about telling others about Jesus.

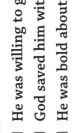

MISSION PASSCARD 9

God can do miracles anytime and anyplace.

Peter

- He was willing to go to jail.
- God saved him with a miracle.
- He was bold about telling others about Jesus.

MISSION PASSCARD 10

Jim Elliot (1927–1956)

- He followed God's plan for his life.
- He was not afraid to die; he knew he would go to heaven.
- He was willing to risk everything to follow God.

Some missionaries give their lives so others can hear about God.

MISSION PASSCARD 10

James

- He followed God's plan for his life.
- He was not afraid to die; he knew he would go to heaven.
- He was willing to risk all to follow God.

Some missionaries give their lives so others can hear about God.

MISSION PASSCARD 11

Hudson Taylor

- This missionary learned from others.
- This missionary did a training program.
- This missionary wanted to tell people in China about Jesus.

Missionaries train to serve God well.

MISSION PASSCARD 11

Timothy

- He was not perfect; he made mistakes.
- He was willing to learn from other missionaries.
- He wanted to tell people about Jesus.

Missionaries train to serve God well.

MISSION PASSCARD 12

Name: _____

- They chose to leave their home and live in a foreign city.
- They want to help people grow in their knowledge of God.
- They want others to know about God.

Some missionaries spend many years in a foreign country.

MISSION PASSCARD 12

Titus

- He chose to leave home and live in a foreign city.
- He wanted to help people grow in their knowledge of God.
- He wanted others to know about God.

Some missionaries spend many years in a foreign country.

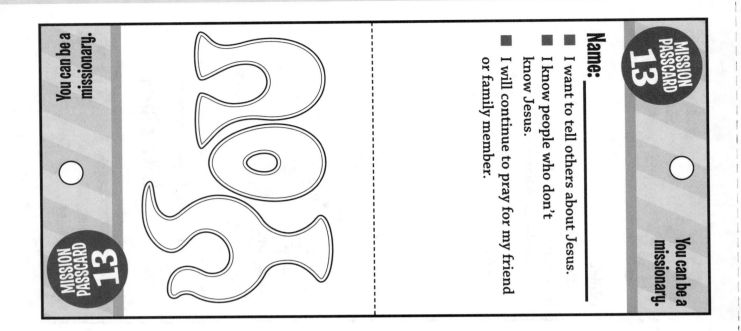

Transformation Bookmark (Lesson 2)

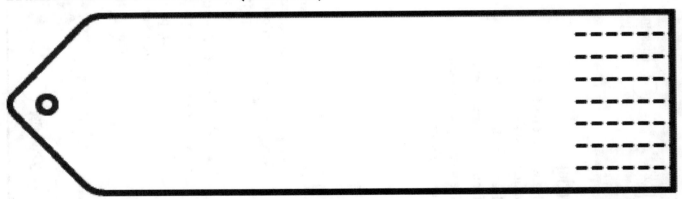

Decode-a-Message (Lesson 7)

Secret Message

$$\overline{19}\ \overline{15}\ \overline{12}\ \overline{22}\ \overline{5}\quad \overline{20}\ \overline{8}\ \overline{9}\ \overline{19}\quad \overline{20}\ \overline{8}\ \overline{5}\ \overline{14}\quad \overline{3}\ \overline{15}\ \overline{13}\ \overline{5}$$

$$\overline{21}\ \overline{16}\quad \overline{6}\ \overline{18}\ \overline{15}\ \overline{14}\ \overline{20}\quad \overline{1}\ \overline{14}\ \overline{4}\quad \overline{16}\ \overline{9}\ \overline{3}\ \overline{11}$$

$$\overline{15}\ \overline{21}\ \overline{20}\quad \overline{1}\quad \overline{3}\ \overline{15}\ \overline{15}\ \overline{11}\ \overline{9}\ \overline{5}!$$

Use this code to find the hidden message.

A=1; B=2; C=3; D=4; E=5; F=6; G=7; H=8; I=9; J=10; K=11; L=12; M=13; N=14; O=15; P=16; Q=17; R=18; S=19; T=20; U=21; V=22; W=23; X=24; Y=25; Z=26; #1=A; 0=B; 2=C; 3=D; 4=E; 5=F; 6=G;

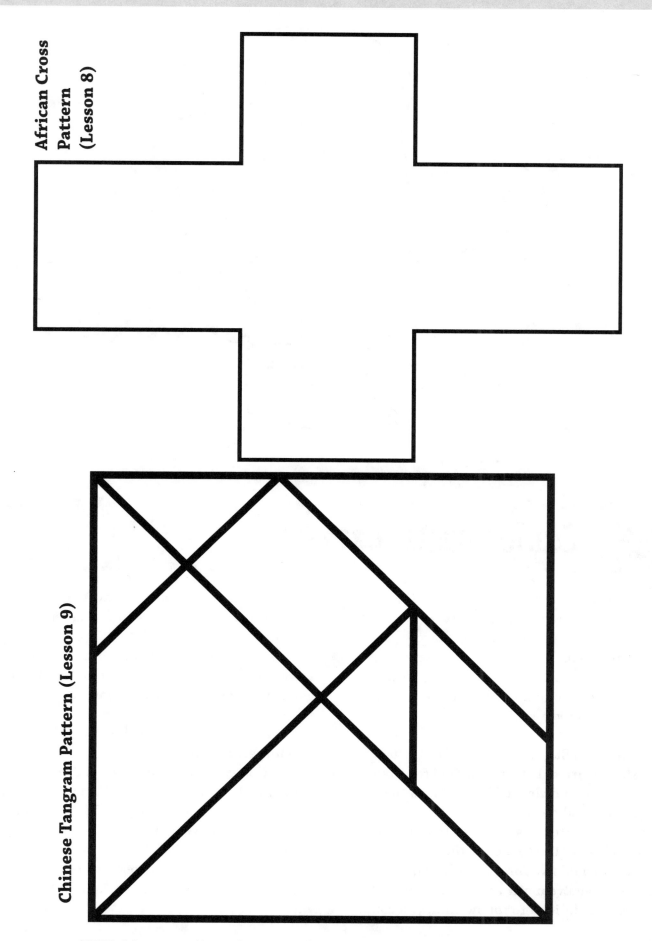

African Cross Pattern (Lesson 8)

Chinese Tangram Pattern (Lesson 9)

Parrot Pattern (Lesson 10)

StationMaster Card #1

This week children learned from Mark 6:7-13 that *missionaries are followers of Jesus who tell others about Him.* You will now lead your group in prayer according to the imPACT model (Praise, Ask, Confess, and Thank). As your children engage in these four activities of prayer, you can further focus their thoughts on today's lesson:

■ *Praise.* **Do you have a voice and hands that can share Christ? Let's praise God for the abilities and knowledge He's given us to let people know about Him.**

■ *Ask.* **Jesus wanted His disciples to tell others that God sent Him to die for their sins so that they could live forever with God in heaven. If you've never accepted Jesus' gift for you and decided to follow Him, you can**

do it now. Lead students who acknowledge this desire in a prayer of confession and submission to Christ.

■ *Confess.* **Our natural way is to think of ourselves and not think about others. We all forget that many people don't know who Jesus is, and we don't think to tell them. Let's tell God we're sorry for thinking of ourselves and forgetting about others.**

■ *Thank.* **God gave us Jesus, His Good News, for everyone.** Have students thank God for the Good News that Jesus died for their sins so that they can live with God in heaven.

Remember that no child should be forced to pray, but do encourage and invite each one. After praying, talk quietly with the children until the next activity.

StationMaster Card #2

This week children learned from the book of Acts and the life of Adoniram Judson that *God can make unbelievers into missionaries.*

You will now lead your group in prayer according to the imPACT model (Praise, Ask, Confess, and Thank). As your children engage in these four activities of prayer, you can further focus their thoughts on today's lesson:

■ *Praise.* **In our Bible story today, we saw how Paul had a plan for his life, but God had a better plan for him.** Give students time to praise God for knowing the perfect plan for their lives.

■ *Ask.* **How did God get Paul's attention? God wants our attention, too.** Have students ask God how He would like them to be his followers at home, school, etc.

■ *Confess.* **Paul was hurting Jesus when he was throwing Christians into jail. Are there things that you do that hurt Jesus?** Allow students to ask forgiveness for specific acts or words that hurt Jesus. They can pray silently or out loud.

■ *Thank.* Encourage children to thank God for the great love that He has for them. He loves them so much He wants them to be with Him forever.

Remember that no child should be forced to pray, but do encourage and invite each one. After praying, talk quietly with the children until the next activity.

StationMaster Card #3

This week children found out from Acts 16:16-36 that *God gives missionaries the strength to keep on even in hard times.*

You will now lead your group in prayer according to the imPACT model (Praise, Ask, Confess, and Thank). As your children engage in these four activities of prayer, you can further focus their thoughts on today's lesson:

■ *Praise.* **Silas went through a difficult time. How did he react to being in prison? He prayed and sang praises!** Allow students to praise God for His care, presence, and help when they've had a hard time recently.

■ *Ask.* **Mary might not have wanted to get in the middle of the warriors' battle, but she went anyway. She got wisdom from God to know what to do.** Lead students in asking God for wisdom to know how to handle something hard or uncomfortable.

■ *Confess.* Encourage children to ask forgiveness for any attitudes that have been sour, unwilling, or uncooperative.

■ *Thank.* **Mary and Silas both had lots of reasons to thank God. They saw Him lead them in the right direction during their hard times.** Students can thank God about ways they've experienced His help or strength recently.

Remember that no child should be forced to pray, but do encourage and invite each one. After praying, talk quietly with the children until the next activity.

StationMaster Card #4

This week children learned that *missionaries work together to get the job done*. The Bible passage came from Acts 16:1-4; Romans 16:21; 1 Corinthians 4:17; 2 Corinthians 1:1; 1 Thessalonians 3:1-4; and 1 Timothy 1:3-4.

You will now lead your group in prayer according to the imPACT model (Praise, Ask, Confess, and Thank). As your children engage in these four activities of prayer, you can further focus their thoughts on today's lesson:

- *Praise.* Give students opportunity to praise God for the help they receive from others.
- *Ask.* **Cook Communication Ministries knows that if they help other publishers, God's Word will reach even more people.** Have students ask God to show or tell them how they might do something to help a missionary.
- *Confess.* **We have the chance to help others, just like missionaries do. If you've made a bad choice and not helped someone when you could have, you can ask God's forgiveness right now.**
- *Thank.* **Missionaries go all over the world to give everyone the chance to know and follow Jesus. Let's thank God for the missionaries we know or those from our church.** If you know no missionaries by name, thank God for Cook Communications and other groups that work together for God.

Remember that no child should be forced to pray, but do encourage and invite each one. After praying, talk quietly with the children until the next activity.

StationMaster Card #5

This week, children learned from Acts 6:1-10 that *missionaries can tell people about God wherever they live.* You will now lead your group in prayer according to the imPACT model (Praise, Ask, Confess, and Thank). As your children engage in these four activities of prayer, you can further focus their thoughts on today's lesson:

- *Praise.* **God showed Stephen how to be a missionary in Jerusalem, and lots of people learned about Jesus through Stephen's obedience.** Lead children in praising God for the people who have shared Jesus with them and taught them about Him.
- *Ask.* **George Mueller didn't travel out of his country to be a missionary. Let's ask God to help us share Jesus in our own neighborhoods.**
- *Confess.* **Stephen's work was to make sure food was passed out fairly. He didn't want the most important job. He was happy to do the work God showed him to do.** Encourage children to talk to God about their own attitudes toward work at home or school. Ask His forgiveness for times of complaining or grumbling.
- *Thank.* **George Mueller learned that God would put him where He needed him.** Model for children a prayer of thankfulness that God loves them and wants only what's best for them. End your time of prayer by thanking Him for each child in your group.

Remember that no child should be forced to pray, but do encourage and invite each one. After praying, talk quietly with the children until the next activity.

StationMaster Card #6

This week children learned from the book of Acts that *God loves to encourage His missionaries.*

You will now lead your group in prayer according to the imPACT model (Praise, Ask, Confess, and Thank). As your children engage in these four activities of prayer, you can further focus their thoughts on today's lesson:

■ *Praise.* **In our Bible passage, we saw how God encouraged both Paul and John Mark through Barnabas.** Students can praise God for giving the gift of encouragement to people.

■ *Ask.* **God can use you to encourage missionaries and other people, too.** Let

children ask God to help them be encouragers.

■ *Confess.* **Barnabas could have discouraged John Mark, but he chose to encourage him.** Give children time to ask God for forgiveness for times they've discouraged others instead of encouraging them.

■ *Thank.* **Remember how God provided others with the same dream as Betty Greene and then gave them an airplane? What can you thank God for today?**

Remember that no child should be forced to pray, but do encourage and invite each one. After praying, talk quietly with the children until the next activity.

StationMaster Card #7

This week children learned from Luke 1:1-4; Acts 1:1-2; and Acts 20:5-12 *that some missionaries write down God's Word for others to read.* You will now lead your group in prayer according to the imPACT model (Praise, Ask, Confess, and Thank). As your children engage in these four activities of prayer, you can further focus their thoughts on today's lesson:

■ *Praise.* **Missionaries sometimes write God's Word in other languages so people can read the Bible in their own language. Let's praise God for being able to read His Word in our language.**

■ *Ask.* Let students ask God to send missionaries to translate His Word in places where the people don't have Bibles yet.

■ *Confess.* **Luke wrote down God's Word so we can read it. We don't always make time to read God's Word.** Students confess their lack of attention to reading the Bible.

■ *Thank.* **We can thank God for the work of people like Luke and Cameron Townsend.** Ask children to name other missionaries they know. Thank God for their hard work for Him. End your time of prayer by thanking Him for each child in your group and His plan to use them for His purposes.

Remember that no child should be forced to pray, but do encourage and invite each one. After praying, talk quietly with the children until the next activity.

StationMaster Card #8

This week children learned from Acts 8:26-40 that *some missionaries go on short journeys.*

You will now lead your group in prayer according to the imPACT model (Praise, Ask, Confess, and Thank). As your children engage in these four activities of prayer, you can further focus their thoughts on today's lesson:

- *Praise.* **God directed Philip to reach an Ethiopian man.** Have students praise God for His deep love for every person and His desire for everyone to receive eternal life.
- *Ask. (missionary)* **is one short-term missionary who God uses to spread the message about Jesus and His gift of salvation. Let's ask God** to give missionaries many opportunities to tell people about Jesus.
- *Confess.* **Like Philip, we should be listening to hear God's voice and obeying Him. This is a time you can tell God you're sorry for times you haven't listened to Him or obeyed.**
- *Thank.* **Someone told you about why Jesus died and that your sins could be forgiven. Right now, thank God for that person who shared about Jesus with you.**

Remember that no child should be forced to pray, but do encourage and invite each one. After praying, talk quietly with the children until the next activity.

StationMaster Card #9

This week children learned from Acts 12:4-17 that *God can do miracles anytime and anyplace.* You will now lead your group in prayer according to the imPACT model (Praise, Ask, Confess, and Thank). As your children engage in these four activities of prayer, you can further focus their thoughts on today's lesson:

- *Praise.* **God showed Peter and Jonathan Goforth that He is bigger than any problem.** Have students praise God for being all powerful and able to do what is impossible for us.
- *Ask.* **The Goforth family didn't die in an attack because God did a miracle. He put the the soldiers to sleep and sent the oxen in the right direction.** Lead students in praying for God's miraculous protection over every missionary.
- *Confess.* **When our problems look as big as Peter's looked, we might trust something besides God to help us. Right now we can each tell God we're sorry for trusting other people or things when we need His power instead.** Allow time for students to confess silently or out loud.
- *Thank.* Model a prayer of thanksgiving to God that He teaches us by the way He works in other people's lives. Encourage children to give thanks for specific ways God has cared for them.

Remember that no child should be forced to pray, but do encourage and invite each one. After praying, talk quietly with the children until the next activity.

StationMaster Card #10

This week children learned from various Bible passages that *some missionaries give their lives so others can hear about God*. You will now lead your group in prayer according to the imPACT model (Praise, Ask, Confess, and Thank). As your children engage in these four activities of prayer, you can focus their thoughts on today's lesson:

- *Praise.* **James followed God's plan.** Have students praise God that He knows everything.
- *Ask.* **Jim Elliot prayed to find out what God wanted him to do next. We can also ask God to show us what He wants us to do.** Students can ask God to show them which direction He wants them to go every day.
- *Confess.* **Fear can make us afraid to do hard things. Let's tell God we're sorry for times we've let our fears stop us when we should have kept going.**
- *Thank.* **James and Jim Elliot gave their most important thing—their lives—so others could find God. Lead students in thanking God for people who are good examples to us.** Encourage children to name people they're thankful for. End your time of prayer by thanking Him for each child in your group. Remember that no child should be forced to pray, but do encourage and invite each one. After praying, talk quietly with the children until the next activity.

StationMaster Card #11

This week children learned from 2 Timothy 2:1-7 that *missionaries train to serve God well*. You will now lead your group in prayer according to the imPACT model (Praise, Ask, Confess, and Thank). As your children engage in these four activities of prayer, you can further focus their thoughts on today's lesson:

- *Praise.* **Both Hudson Taylor and Timothy showed many people who Jesus is. Missionaries today are doing that everyday, too. Let's praise God for the way He is giving many people eternal life through the work of missionaries all over the world.** If you or the children know missionaries by name, they can include them specifically in this praise time.
- *Ask.* **Both the missionaries we studied today were willing to learn what God wanted them to learn. He wants you and me to learn more about Him too, even if we don't move to a different country to serve Him.** Students can ask the Holy Spirit to teach them more about God and living for Him.
- *Confess.* **Have you ever not wanted to learn what you needed to learn? Even when we don't do what we should do, God loves us.** Lead children in praying for forgiveness for their times of disobedience or unwillingness to learn and practice godliness.
- *Thank.* **We all learn because someone teaches us. This a time for you to thank God for someone who has taught you, at home, at school or at church.** End your time of prayer by thanking Him for each child in your group. Remember that no child should be forced to pray, but do encourage and invite each one. After praying, talk quietly with the children until the next activity.

StationMaster Card #12

This week children learned from the book of Titus that *some missionaries spend many years in a foreign country*. You will now lead your group in prayer according to the imPACT model (Praise, Ask, Confess, and Thank). As your children engage in these four activities of prayer, you can further focus their thoughts on today's lesson:

- *Praise.* **God used Titus to show His love to the people on the island of Crete.** Have students praise God for ways He has shown love to them recently.
- *Ask.* **We don't have to be grown ups to be missionaries. Right in our own neighborhoods and schools we can share Jesus.** Have children ask God to direct their steps so that they will tell people about Him.
- *Confess.* **Titus was more concerned about the people of Crete than about himself. We can be too concerned about ourselves and forget the needs of others.** Allow students a chance to ask for forgiveness for time when they did not care about others' needs.
- *Thank.* **What do you want to thank God for today?** Have students thank God for specific gifts or ways He has cared for them.

Remember that no child should be forced to pray, but do encourage and invite each one. After praying, talk quietly with the children until the next activity.

StationMaster Card #13

This week children learned that *you and I can be missionaries*, too. You will now lead your group in prayer according to the imPACT model (Praise, Ask, Confess, and Thank). As your children engage in these four activities of prayer, you can further focus their thoughts on today's lesson:

- *Praise.* **It's amazing how much God loves every person. That's why He so much wants every person to trust in Jesus.** Lead students in praising God for His unconditional love for them and others.
- *Ask.* **Who might you tell about Jesus this week?** Allow a quiet moment as children seek God's wisdom in who they can talk to this week. Then let children pray aloud as they choose.
- *Confess.* **What feelings or things stop us from sharing Jesus with others?** After children offer their insights, ask them to confess the ones they're guilty of, and receive forgiveness.
- *Thank.* **God loves each person so much that He will forgive them every time they ask for forgiveness.** Have students thank God for His forgiveness. Go around the group one more time to thank God that they've been given the gift of eternal life and a place in God's family. End your time of prayer by thanking Him for each child in your group.

Remember that no child should be forced to pray, but do encourage and invite each one. After praying, talk quietly with the children until the next activity.

MISSION ADVENTURE FILES

Directions: Each of these "missions" should be copied onto separate sheets of paper and placed inside a multi-pocket file portfolio, each in its own pocket.

Your mission is to discover what makes a good missionary.

Mission One:
- ■ Learn what the word "missionary" means.

Your mission is to discover what makes a good missionary.

Mission Two:
- ■ Find out if God can use unbelievers.
- ■ *Study* Paul and Adoniram Judson.

Your mission is to discover what makes a good missionary.

Mission Three:
- ■ Find out where missionaries find strength when things get hard.
- ■ *Study* Silas and Mary Slessor.

Your mission is to discover what makes a good missionary.

Mission Four:
- ■ Find out if missionaries work together or alone.
- ■ *Study* Timothy and Cook Communications Ministries International.

Your mission is to discover what makes a good missionary.

Mission Five:
- ■ Find out where missionaries are working.
- ■ *Study* Stephen and George Mueller.

Your mission is to discover what makes a good missionary.

Mission Six:
- ■ Find out what keeps missionaries going.
- ■ *Study* Barnabas and Betty Greene.

Your mission is to discover what makes a good missionary.

Mission Seven:
- ■ Find out about one task some missionaries do.
- ■ *Study* Luke and Cameron Townsend.

Your mission is to discover what makes a good missionary.

Mission Eight:
- ■ Find out if mission trips are long or short.
- ■ *Study* Philip and a *local, short-term missionary*.

Your mission is to discover what makes a good missionary.

Mission Nine:
- ■ Find out if God ever uses special power to help missionaries.
- ■ *Study* Peter and Jonathan Goforth.

Your mission is to discover what makes a good missionary.

Mission Ten:
- ■ Find out what some missionaries give up to tell others about Jesus.
- ■ *Study* James and Jim Elliot.

Your mission is to discover what makes a good missionary.

Mission Eleven:
- ■ Find out how missionaries train for their jobs.
- ■ *Study* Timothy and Hudson Taylor.

Your mission is to discover what makes a good missionary.

Mission Twelve:
- ■ Find out if mission trips are long or short.
- ■ *Study* Titus and a *church-sponsored missionary family*.

Your mission is to discover what makes a good missionary.

Mission Thirteen:
- ■ Find out who is a missionary.
- ■ Review all the missionaries studied in this unit.

(Dear Children's Ministry Leader: The following letter should be set up so it can be copied on church letterhead and sent or e-mailed to a church-sponsored, missionary family. Please be sensitive to Christian language that could put your missionary in jeopardy. Change the letter accordingly.)

Dear *(name of church-sponsored missionary family),*

For thirteen weeks, our children's ministry will be learning about missions. Our goal is to discover what makes a good missionary and to help children learn that everyone of us can tell others about Jesus, whether in our neighborhoods or across the world.

During this time, we will be talking about how some missionaries leave their homes to live among people who need to know Him. We will be studying the book of Titus from the Bible and how Titus helped the churches in Crete grow. During this lesson, we would also like to tell about a missionary family.

Would you be willing to provide us with information about what you and your family do as missionaries? Our focus for that class will be how people minister to non-Christians and Christians wherever God sends them. Also, if you have time and resources, it would be especially meaningful to the children to receive a video from you. You might include: your family, your surroundings, details about what you do, or things we can pray about for you.

If you could send us a letter, an e-mail, or a video by *(give a date),* we would appreciate it so much. Please let me know as soon as possible if you would like to participate with our children in this exciting exploration of missions. Thank you for considering our request. Please feel free to contact me with any questions.

In His Name,

Leave room for a signature
Phone number
E-mail address

Dear Parents,

During the next thirteen weeks in children's ministry, your child will learn about missions as we investigate the lives and work of real Bible-time and modern-day missionaries. Our *Sharing God with Others* curriculum will help children understand that they too can tell others about Jesus. God can use them to bring the Good News of Jesus Christ to their schools, neighborhoods, and families.

Playing the role of a secret agent, your child will be given a weekly mission to discover *what makes a good missionary*. They will search the Bible for answers and learn how those Bible truths apply to their own worlds. To build the drama of this mission, we will fingerprint and photograph children during the first class to make Mission I.D. cards. If you would prefer your child not to participate in this activity, please discuss this with me before the first week of class.

When Jesus told his disciples to "Go . . . and make disciples of all the nations," there was no age limit! The Great Commission is given to all believers, no matter how young or old. Because this is such an important message, your child will receive a take-home paper for each lesson, designed to support the Bible Truth for that day. These take-home papers will include fun activities, a Bible memory verse, and a challenge to pray with you for real missionaries in real places on a mission!

If you have any questions about our study about Sharing God with Others, please feel free to bring them to discuss them with the children's ministry leaders. We are excited about what God is doing in the lives of our children and would appreciate your prayers for the teachers and children.

In His Name,

Bible Truth

Missionaries are followers of Jesus who tell others about Him.

Memory Verse

Therefore <u>go</u> and make disciples of all nations, <u>baptizing</u> them in the name of the <u>Father</u> and of the <u>Son</u> and of the Holy Spirit (Matthew 28:19).

Your Turn

Show God's compassion to others. With an adult, prepare a jug of a tasty drink. Take the drink and some cups and find some road workers, fire or police workers, or homeless people in your area. Offer them a drink and a smile.

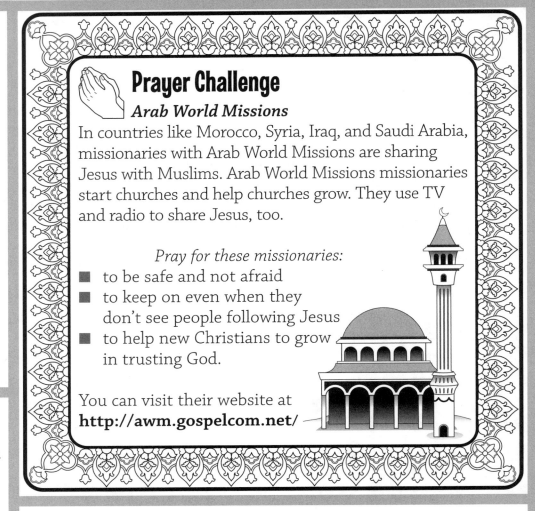

Prayer Challenge

Arab World Missions

In countries like Morocco, Syria, Iraq, and Saudi Arabia, missionaries with Arab World Missions are sharing Jesus with Muslims. Arab World Missions missionaries start churches and help churches grow. They use TV and radio to share Jesus, too.

Pray for these missionaries:
- to be safe and not afraid
- to keep on even when they don't see people following Jesus
- to help new Christians to grow in trusting God.

You can visit their website at
http://awm.gospelcom.net/

Coded Message

Write the first letter of the word of each picture on the line below to discover a secret message.

Dear Parents and Guardians,

Please check off the items your child completed this week:

- ☐ Prayer Challenge
- ☐ Coded Message
- ☐ Memory Verse
- ☐ Your Turn

Adult Signature:

FAST TRACK! TICKET

On the Fast Track!

Bible Truth

God can turn unbelievers into missionaries.

Memory Verse

Teaching them to <u>obey</u> everything I have <u>commanded</u> you. And surely I am with you <u>always</u>, to the very <u>end</u> of the age (Matthew 28:20).

Your Turn

Make a colorful card of encouragement to send to a missionary family. Tell them who you are and draw a picture of yourself. Pray for this family before you send the card. Ask someone at church or visit the International Ministries website above if you don't know who to send your card to.

Prayer Challenge

International Ministries

When Adoniram Judson became a Christian, he went to Burma as a missionary. International Missions still shares Jesus in Burma and other Asian countries. They care for the sick, respond to disasters, and help churches grow.

You can pray for these missionaries:

■ to be good examples of God's love
■ to have strength and safety in emergencies

Their website: **www.internationalministries.org**

Maze

Draw a line to show this child how to find Jesus.

START

END

Dear Parents and Guardians,

Please check off the items your child completed this week:

☐ Prayer Challenge
☐ Maze
☐ Memory Verse
☐ Your Turn

Adult Signature:

FAST TRACK! TICKET

On the Fast Track!

Bible Truth

God gives missionaries strength to keep on even in hard times.

Memory Verse

He gives <u>strength</u> to the <u>weary</u> and increases the <u>power</u> of the <u>weak</u> (Isaiah 40:29).

Your Turn

Ask for a jar to start a coin collection for missions work. Invite people in your family to put their extra coins in the jar. When it is full, give the collected coins to your church to send to the missionaries they support.

Prayer Challenge

Serving In Mission (SIM)

God gave Silas and Mary Slessor strength in hard times. Mary was a missionary in Nigeria. Today, SIM has many missionaries in Nigeria. They give medical care, start new churches, help people learn how to follow Jesus, and teach children.

Pray for these missionaries:

- ◼ to encourage Christians in Nigeria to love others
- ◼ to be strong when there is opposition
- ◼ to train Nigerians into church leaders

You can visit their website: **www.sim.org**

Word Search

See how many of the following words that mean "hard" you can find in this puzzle. Circle the words as you find them:

difficult, tricky, tough, demanding, testing, challenging, harsh, strict, fierce, relentless, complicated, complex, trying, grim, bad

```
C D E D E M A N D I N G
E C R E I F F T O U G H
M O E T F F I T S G N K
O M L A K J F C I H I Y
S P E C L G R I M B G K
E L N I G N I R C R N C
L E T L N I G T H U E I
B X L P I T I S A T L R
U M E M L S D N R A L T
O P S O E E O Y S L A B
R Q S C U T I R H S H A
T V U T R N L E U R C D
W X A Y G S U O U D R A
```

Dear Parents and Guardians,

Please check off the items your child completed this week:

- ☐ Prayer Challenge
- ☐ Word Search
- ☐ Memory Verse
- ☐ Your Turn

Adult Signature:

FAST TRACK! TICKET

On the Fast Track!

Bible Truth

Missionaries work together to get the job done.

Memory Verse

<u>Two</u> are better than <u>one</u>, because they have a good <u>return</u> for their <u>work</u> (Ecclesiastes 4:9).

Your Turn

From your own books, choose one or more that you don't read anymore. Make sure it's in good shape. In the phone book or through your church, find a shelter for homeless or needy children, or a foster child program. Give them your book to give to children who have none of their own.

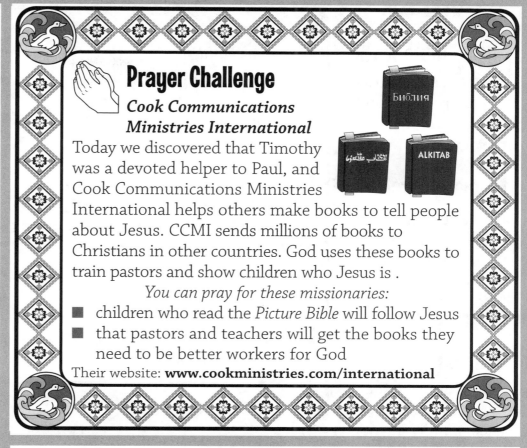

Prayer Challenge

Cook Communications Ministries International

Today we discovered that Timothy was a devoted helper to Paul, and Cook Communications Ministries International helps others make books to tell people about Jesus. CCMI sends millions of books to Christians in other countries. God uses these books to train pastors and show children who Jesus is .

You can pray for these missionaries:
- children who read the *Picture Bible* will follow Jesus
- that pastors and teachers will get the books they need to be better workers for God

Their website: **www.cookministries.com/international**

Hidden Picture

Find 10 Bibles hidden in the picture. Color them in and imagine them in 10 different countries where they could be given to people who don't have a Bible.

Dear Parents and Guardians,

Please check off the items your child completed this week:

- ☐ Prayer Challenge
- ☐ Hidden Picture
- ☐ Memory Verse
- ☐ Your Turn

Adult Signature:

FAST TRACK! TICKET

Bible Truth

Missionaries can tell people about God wherever they live.

Memory Verse

Dear <u>children</u>, let us not <u>love</u> with words or <u>tongue</u> but with actions and in truth (1 John 3:18).

Your Turn

Show your care for an elderly person or needy family in your neighborhood. Make some cookies or a loaf of bread, wrap it nicely and make a gift tag with a friendly greeting, like "God loves you, and we do, too." Deliver your gift with a smile.

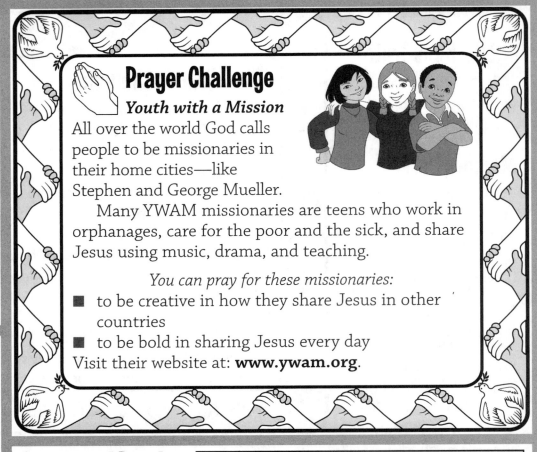

Prayer Challenge

Youth with a Mission

All over the world God calls people to be missionaries in their home cities—like Stephen and George Mueller.

Many YWAM missionaries are teens who work in orphanages, care for the poor and the sick, and share Jesus using music, drama, and teaching.

You can pray for these missionaries:

- to be creative in how they share Jesus in other countries
- to be bold in sharing Jesus every day

Visit their website at: **www.ywam.org**.

Crossword Puzzle

Find where these words go in the puzzle.

- Stephen
- serve
- action
- missionaries
- bold
- pray
- neighbor

Dear Parents and Guardians,

Please check off the items your child completed this week:

- ❑ Prayer Challenge
- ❑ Crossword
- ❑ Memory Verse
- ❑ Your Turn

Adult Signature:

_____

FAST TRACK! TICKET

On the Fast Track!

Bible Truth

God loves to encourage His missionaries.

Memory Verse

The LORD your God is with you, he is mighty to save. He will take great delight in you, he will quiet you with his love, he will rejoice over you with singing (Zephaniah 3:17).

Early elementary verse in *bold* type.

Your Turn

Volunteer in a community project to show you care for those around you. You can pick up litter on your street, feed the birds in your neighborhood, or plant some flowers in front of your church.

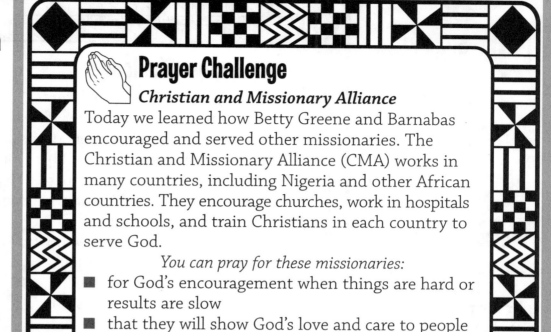

Prayer Challenge

Christian and Missionary Alliance

Today we learned how Betty Greene and Barnabas encouraged and served other missionaries. The Christian and Missionary Alliance (CMA) works in many countries, including Nigeria and other African countries. They encourage churches, work in hospitals and schools, and train Christians in each country to serve God.

You can pray for these missionaries:

■ for God's encouragement when things are hard or results are slow

■ that they will show God's love and care to people

You can visit their website at: **www.cmalliance.org**

Paul and Barnabas Copy-It Picture:

Draw a 10 X 10 grid on white paper with 1/2" squares. Then, look at each box below and copy what you see into the same square on the new grid. Once you complete each box, you will have drawn the whole picture. *(Optional)* Instead, you may color the picture on this page.

Dear Parents and Guardians,

Please check off the items your child completed this week:

❏ Prayer Challenge
❏ Copy-it Picture
❏ Memory Verse
❏ Your Turn

Adult Signature:

FAST TRACK! TICKET

On the Fast Track!

Bible Truth

Some missionaries write down God's Word for others to read.

Memory Verse

Your <u>word</u> is a lamp to my <u>feet</u> and a <u>light</u> for my path (Psalms 119:105).

Prayer Challenge

Wycliffe Bible Translators

Today we discovered that Luke wrote his Gospel for us to read and Cameron Townsend translated the Bible into other languages. Wycliffe Bible Translators has put the Bible into 100s of languages, so people all over the world can read the Bible in their own language.

You can pray that:

- Bible translators will know how to make the words just right
- people who read the Bible in their language will understand it and believe

Their website: **www.wycliffe.org**

Your Turn

You too can write verses of the Bible for others to read. Copy John 3:16 (or other verses you like) on several blank sheets of paper. Use interesting type and decorate the empty part of the papers with colorful pictures too. Give these Bible verses to people you know, or post them where others will see.

Dear Parents and Guardians,

Please check off the items your child completed this week:

- ☐ Prayer Challenge
- ☐ Hidden Picture
- ☐ Memory Verse
- ☐ Your Turn

Adult Signature:

FAST TRACK! TICKET

Hidden Picture

Find these things in the picture: a greeting card, Bible, praying hands, pen, pencil, desk, glasses, books, and lamp.

On the Fast Track!

Bible Truth

Missionaries sometimes go on short journeys.

Memory Verse

Be <u>kind</u> and compassionate to one another, forgiving each other, just as in <u>Christ</u> God forgave <u>you</u>. (Ephesians 4:32).

Your Turn

Do acts of kindness for people in your family. You might do your sister's or brother's chores without saying anything. Find a way to serve your parents as a surprise. When they say thank you, tell them you're showing care in the name of Jesus.

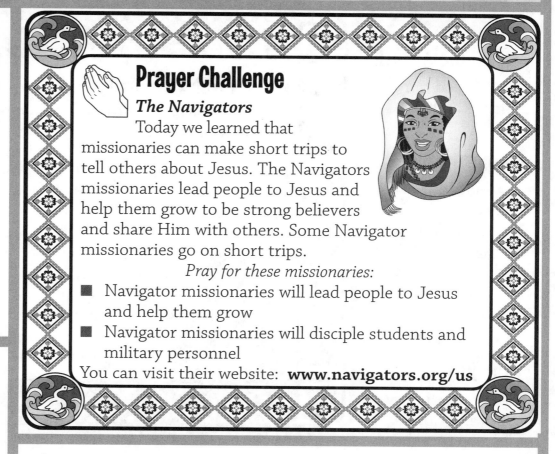

Prayer Challenge

The Navigators

Today we learned that missionaries can make short trips to tell others about Jesus. The Navigators missionaries lead people to Jesus and help them grow to be strong believers and share Him with others. Some Navigator missionaries go on short trips.

Pray for these missionaries:

- Navigator missionaries will lead people to Jesus and help them grow
- Navigator missionaries will disciple students and military personnel

You can visit their website: **www.navigators.org/us**

Morse Code

Below is the Morse Code. This is the way people communicate with lights or over telegraph lines. Study the code. Write this week's verse in Morse Code in the space below or on another paper.

A ._	**B** _...	**C** _._.	**D** _..	**E** .	**F** .._.
G __.	**H**	**I** ..	**J** .___	**K** _._	**L** ._..
M __	**N** _.	**O** ___	**P** .__.	**Q** __._	**R** ._.
S ...	**T** _	**U** .._	**V** ..._	**W** .__	**X** _.._
Y _.__	**Z** __..				

Dear Parents and Guardians,

Please check off the items your child completed this week:

- ❑ Prayer Challenge
- ❑ Morse Code
- ❑ Memory Verse
- ❑ Your Turn

Adult Signature:

FAST TRACK! TICKET

On the Fast Track!

Bible Truth

God can do miracles anytime and anyplace.

Memory Verse

Jesus looked at them and said, "With <u>man</u> this is <u>impossible</u>, but with <u>God</u> all things are <u>possible</u>" (Matthew 19:26).

Your Turn

Clean out your toy boxes and closets. Clean up toys that are in good shape and donate them to a homeless shelter that serves families or a hospital. Before you go, pray that God will use your toys to give children happiness even when their lives are difficult.

Prayer Challenge

Far East Broadcasting company (FEBC)

God performed a miracle to save the life of Jonathan Goforth in Asia. FEBC works in Asia making radio programs in 154 languages. People who can't go to church or who don't have a Bible can learn about God by listening to these radio programs.

You can pray for these missionaries:

- that many people will listen and believe in Jesus
- that speakers of other languages will want to make radio programs for their own people

Their website is: **www.febc.org**

Secret Message

Match the numbers to letters and decode this secret message.

1	2	3	4	5	6	7	8	9	10	11	12	13
A	B	C	D	E	F	G	H	I	J	K	L	M

14	15	16	17	18	19	20	21	22	23	24	25	26
N	O	P	Q	R	S	T	U	V	W	X	Y	Z

_ _ _ _ _ _ _ _ _ _ _ _ _ _
1 14 4 23 9 20 8 15 21 20 6 1 9 20 8

_ _ _ _ _ _ _ _ _ _ _ _ _ _ _ _
9 20 9 19 9 13 16 15 19 19 9 2 12 5

_ _ _ _ _ _ _ _ _
20 15 16 12 5 1 19 5 .

_ _ _
7 15 4

_ _ _ _ _ _ _ _ 11:6a.
8 5 2 18 5 23 19

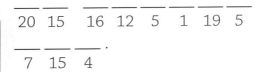

FAST TRACK! TICKET

On the Fast Track!

Bible Truth

Some missionaries give their lives so others can hear about God.

Memory Verse

Be <u>strong</u> and courageous. Do not be <u>terrified</u>; do not be discouraged, for the LORD your God will be with <u>you</u> wherever you <u>go</u> (Joshua 1:9).

Prayer Challenge

Mission Aviation Fellowship

MAF provides air travel for missionaries who work in remote and far away places. These pilots deliver supplies and carry people who need medical help.

You can pray:
- for the safety of these pilots, mechanics, families
- that people will see God's love in the missionaries and their caring

You can check out their website at **www.maf.org**

Your Turn

When you hear or see an airplane this week, pray that someone will trust in Jesus today because of the work of MAF or another mission.

Dot-to-Dot

Connect the dots to find one soldier in God's army.

Dear Parents and Guardians,

Please check off the items your child completed this week:

- ❑ Prayer Challenge
- ❑ Dot-to-Dot
- ❑ Memory Verse
- ❑ Your Turn

Adult Signature:

_____

FAST TRACK! TICKET

On the Fast Track!

Bible Truth

Missionaries train to serve God well.

Memory Verse

Train yourself to be godly. (1 Timothy 4:7).

Your Turn

This week, give up something you like to eat often. It can be anything, like candy, cookies, soda, or hamburgers. Ask your mom or dad to put the money they would spend on those treats in a jar. At the end of the week, give this money to your church for a missionary, or send it to a missionary organization you've read about in your *On the Fast Track!* paper.

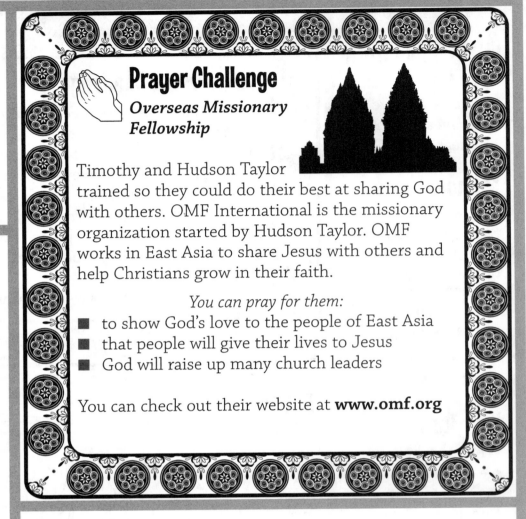

Prayer Challenge
Overseas Missionary Fellowship

Timothy and Hudson Taylor trained so they could do their best at sharing God with others. OMF International is the missionary organization started by Hudson Taylor. OMF works in East Asia to share Jesus with others and help Christians grow in their faith.

You can pray for them:
- to show God's love to the people of East Asia
- that people will give their lives to Jesus
- God will raise up many church leaders

You can check out their website at **www.omf.org**

Training Poster

Get a large sheet of blank paper and draw lines to make four boxes. At the top, write this week's verse in big colorful letters. In each box, draw yourself doing something to train yourself to serve God well, for example, reading your Bible. Label each box.

Dear Parents and Guardians,

Please check off the items your child completed this week:

- ☐ Prayer Challenge
- ☐ Training Poster
- ☐ Memory Verse
- ☐ Your Turn

Adult Signature:

_____

FAST TRACK! TICKET

Train yourself to be godly.
(1 Timothy 4:7)

Read my Bible

On the Fast Track!

📖 Bible Truth

Some missionaries leave their homes for a long time to live with those who don't know Jesus.

Memory Verse

Let your light <u>shine</u> before men, that they may <u>see</u> your good deeds, and praise your <u>Father</u> in <u>heaven</u> (Matthew 5:16).

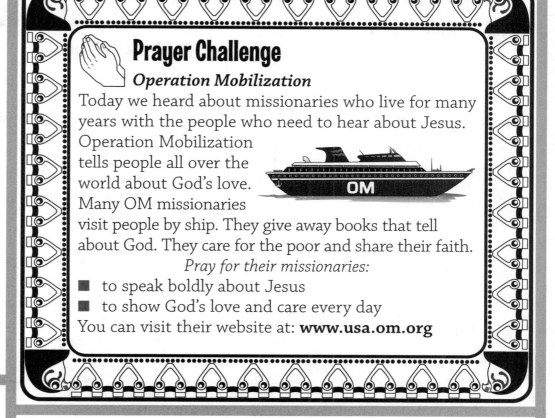

🙏 Prayer Challenge

Operation Mobilization

Today we heard about missionaries who live for many years with the people who need to hear about Jesus. Operation Mobilization tells people all over the world about God's love. Many OM missionaries visit people by ship. They give away books that tell about God. They care for the poor and share their faith.

Pray for their missionaries:
■ to speak boldly about Jesus
■ to show God's love and care every day

You can visit their website at: **www.usa.om.org**

Your Turn

Do an act of good works for your church. You can wash the toys in the nursery, weed the flower beds, wash some windows, stuff envelopes in the office. Do it with joy!

Balloon Buddy

Make a portrait of someone who can tell others about God's love anytime and anyplace. YOU! Trace your feet on a piece of cardboard. Draw on toes or shoes and cut them out. Then blow up a balloon. Draw your head and body on the balloon with permanent markers. Make a small slit in the middle of the feet and poke the knot of the balloon through it.

Dear Parents and Guardians,

Please check off the items your child completed this week:

❏ Prayer Challenge
❏ Balloon Buddy
❏ Memory Verse
❏ Your Turn

Adult Signature:

FAST TRACK! TICKET

On the Fast Track!

Bible Truth

You and I can be a missionaries.

Memory Verse

Then I <u>heard</u> the voice of the Lord saying, "Whom shall I <u>send</u>? And who will go for us?" And I said, "Here am <u>I</u>. <u>Send</u> me!" (Isaiah 6:8)

Your Turn

Ask someone at home to help you collect cans of food to donate to a local relief organization, such as a homeless shelter, a soup kitchen, or an organization your church supports. You might ask several friends to join you doing this. God wants you to serve others right here at home!

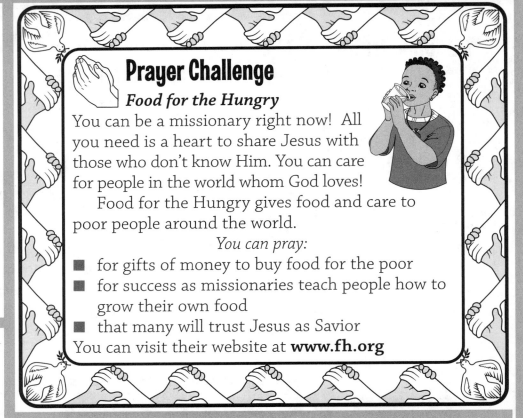

Prayer Challenge

Food for the Hungry

You can be a missionary right now! All you need is a heart to share Jesus with those who don't know Him. You can care for people in the world whom God loves!

Food for the Hungry gives food and care to poor people around the world.

You can pray:

- for gifts of money to buy food for the poor
- for success as missionaries teach people how to grow their own food
- that many will trust Jesus as Savior

You can visit their website at **www.fh.org**

Color Puzzle

Who can be a missionary? Color all the sections with U, Y or O in them.

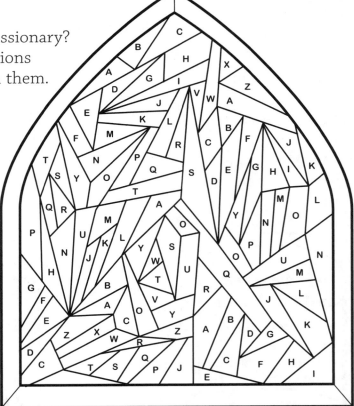

Dear Parents and Guardians,

Please check off the items your child completed this week:

- ☐ Prayer Challenge
- ☐ Color Puzzle
- ☐ Memory Verse
- ☐ Your Turn

Adult Signature:

_____

FAST TRACK! TICKET